The Guts & Glory of Day Trading

True stories of day traders who made (or lost) $1,000,000

By Mark Ingebretsen

HARRIMAN HOUSE LTD

3A Penns Road
Petersfield
Hampshire
GU32 2EW
GREAT BRITAIN

Tel: +44 (0)1730 233870
Fax: +44 (0)1730 233880
Email: enquiries@harriman-house.com
Website: www.harriman-house.com

First published in United States of America in 2001 by Prima Publishing
Reprinted in Great Britain 2010

Copyright © Harriman House Ltd

The right of Mark Ingebretsen to be identified as the author has been asserted
in accordance with the Copyright, Design and Patents Act 1988.

ISBN: 978-190-6659-71-4

British Library Cataloguing in Publication Data
A CIP catalogue record for this book can be obtained from the British Library.

Printed and bound in the UK by CPI Antony Rowe, Chippenham.

To Deanna and Erik

Contents

Foreword

When the market for tech stocks started tanking last spring, I knew it was just a matter of time before the mainstream press would gleefully proclaim the death of day trading.

Day trading has become a dirty word among many financial journalists, who see its practitioners as not only harming themselves and their families but also the markets. Day traders, they believe, roil the markets in ways that make it unstable for the majority of investors.

So, did it happen? Did day trading die? As I write this, the market is in a decided slump, yet I don't for a minute believe that people are losing their interest in the market or in trading and investing online. To find out, I started digging out some statistics, I came up with some conflicting, or at least inconclusive, numbers. U.S. Bancorp Piper Jaffray estimates that more than 2 million online trading accounts were added in the second quarter of 2000, a gain of 12.8 percent. The firm estimates that there are some 11.7 million online investors/traders today. Assets held in online brokerage accounts total more than $1 trillion.

At E*Trade, the average number of trades executed each day during the calendar third quarter fell 11 percent from the second quarter and was way down from its peak. But trades at E*Trade are still up 84 percent from last year's level. The flow of new cash into customer accounts at E*Trade was up 37 percent during the summer quarter, while 337,000 new accounts were opened, down just 1 percent from 1999. But average daily trading volume was down over the same period by about 23 percent.

It's hard to know whether traders are affected more by a down market than the average online investor. At Tradescape, a brokerage with direct-access technology that caters to active traders, the average customer traded more than 547 times in the last quarter, according to U.S. Bancorp Piper Jaffray. But another study by Jupiter Media Metrix shows that the number of visits to online trading sites declined nearly 20 percent in the past six months. On the other hand, interest in the overall category of business and finance sites remains strong: Traffic at these sites is up 11 percent. Judging from the way I see the "trader" and "investor" casually thrown around in the media, however, it's tough to know how accurate these numbers are. Dozens of sites qualify as both investing and trading sites in our estimation, offering information for both the long-term and the short-term market player.

What is a day trader? A widely varied breed. Some trade Monday through Friday from an office, perhaps scalping a few cents off dozens or hundreds of trades in a day, ending up flat at the closing bell. An industry trade group, the Electronic Traders Association, estimates there are only around 5,000 of these "pure" day traders. Others trade at home, using a couple of monitors, a fast Net connection, and direct-access software. They're likely to be studying charts and using screening software after hours to plot the next day's strategy. It's estimated there are around 240,000 of these hyperactive traders. Other trades fall into the momentum camp, buying and holding positions for a few days or weeks instead of hours. Some, such as Bob Martin, profiled here, research and trade part-time, keeping their day jobs.

What is a day trader? Maybe it doesn't matter. Day trader, active trader, online investor – all are harnessing the power of the Internet to take control of their finances. This book would have been unheard of just a few years ago. Though a small number of non-professionals toiled in day trading firms' offices, it was the growth of the Internet, and the tools the Net provides, that made a lot more people realize they could take a crack at trading. There's never been a more exciting time to be in the market. From top-flight screening software to real-time quotes to direct-access brokers and access to real-time news, individuals really can be on an even playing field with professionals. The Securities and Exchange Commission is encouraging the revolution in its way. The SEC's Regulation Fair Disclosure, which went into effect last year, mandates that companies make announcements about operations to all investors via the Internet or other means, not just to a few select analysts.

Is day trading dangerous? That depends on what you compare it to. Last year I heard Harvey Houtkin, the outspoken chairman of All-Tech, a day-trading firm, speaking at a trading expo in Oakland, California. Houtkin, who has been a sharp critic of regulation of the day-trading industry, pounded the podium, wondering why the government doesn't discourage individuals from starting up restaurants. After all, he pointed out, the failure rate for restaurants is quite high. Critics of online trading like to tout the fact that most people who day trade end up losing money. But who are we to say they shouldn't try? Most day-trading firms and direct-access brokers have some sort of qualifications to open an account, requiring as much as $10,000 on deposit, and many also require a training course. Online sources for learning about trading are increasing, and getting better all the time. You can watch experienced traders draw charts at Web sites such as Intelligent Speculator.com and HardRightEdge.com, and you can learn at sites such as TradingMarkets.com.

Whether Wall Street status quo seekers like it or not, on-line trading is here to stay. And who better to profile some of the most interesting players than Mark Ingebretsen. Mark has written for the magazine I edit, *Online Investor*, since the first issue hit newsstands in the summer of 1998. From the beginning, Mark has understood the issues surrounding online investing and trading like few other journalists. For *Online Investor* and TheStreet.com, where he writes a weekly column, Mark has tackled some of the most complicated topics – from options to electronic communications networks to shorting to after-hours trading to how to trade Internet stocks to neural networks. In the course of his reporting, he has interviewed dozens of professional and amateur traders, academics, and online investors.

I admit certain bias. Because I am a financial journalist, and not a trader of financial pro who just happens to edit a magazine, I believe that journalists tend to write the best books and magazine articles about trading. Such is the case with Mark.

Whatever he's writing about, Mark keeps in mind first and foremost the average trader or investor, and tries to fashion strategies that anybody can benefit from. That's why I was excited when I heard he was writing this book. I knew that from every traders' story he elicited he'd get interesting tips and lessons. Mark has an uncanny and rare ability to take complicated topics and boil them down into entertaining, highly readable stories. Mark is passionate about his subject matter, and it shows. The articles he writes are some of the most widely read in our magazine.

Investors and traders aren't likely to lose interest in the access to information, sophisticated charting and financial planning tools, and other benefits of the online investing revolution merely because the market is down. Plus, savvy traders know that down markets can be played just as up markets can, if you know how. The Internet has made it possible. Nothing's going to stop it. Read this book and you'll understand why.

Jan Parr

Editor, *Online Investor*

2001

Preface

For all their trappings of wealth and prestige, today's great exchanges had simple beginnings. The London Stock Exchange began in a pair of coffee houses located along a narrow alley. The New York Stock Exchange evolved from a group of traders who met beneath a buttonwood tree. Both those exchanges allowed traders to look one another in the eye while they haggled over shares in the East India Company and other hot issues of the day.

In the many years since then, technology has radically streamlined the trading process. But the aim of that technology has been the same, to create pools of liquidity large enough to drive the world's economies.

As trading technology evolved, it invented tools that would foreshadow those everyone used years later on the Internet. Before anyone knew anything about Web-style mash-ups, for example, traders staring into their Reuters and Bloomberg terminals could follow the changing prices of stocks, commodities, and currencies as they occurred. At the same time, they could also gaze at news headlines, statistical charts, and weather forecasts in the hopes of forecasting pricing trends. Likewise, before there were social networks, traders mulled over news and rumors in thousands of chat rooms and discussion threads, many of which were devoted to a particular stock or trading style.

Then, in the '90s, when the Web had advanced enough to reliably support online trading, millions of enthusiasts took up day trading. It was absorbing and fun, like gambling, you could do it from the privacy of your home, and it might even make you rich.

The Web has been called a disruptive technology that barrels over established ways of doing business, crushing companies or even entire industries in the process. One of the very first industries the Web challenged was the traditional brokerage. Thanks to online trading, it was no longer necessary to pay high commissions and listen to what many saw as tainted advice.

Traders themselves could research the stocks that interested them and buy and sell shares with a single keystroke. Why wait half a day for your broker to take your call?

With a fast enough Internet connection, those traders could even buy and sell stocks several times over during the course of a day. In doing so, their actions mimicked those of market makers and the trading departments attached to the established brokerages. Without the brokerages' high overhead, traders hunkered over their computer monitors at home were able to scalp profits inside the spreads between the buy and sell prices that the brokerages enjoyed. And in the process, they invented day trading.

Day trading owed its existence to the Internet. But it also fed on the Internet's promise of untold wealth. As day traders became more and more fixated on the computer and Internet sites that provided their livelihood, they also focused on shares of Internet companies they believed would break down other industries in the same way the net had made trading for the masses possible. You could book a plane flight on the net, buy groceries, or search for a new home. Shares of start-up companies launched to perform those tasks quickly soared in price.

Share prices soared because those Internet companies were invariably small, and they had relatively few shares to trade. Thus, when large sums of money from day traders poured in to buy, demand and astronomical price levels quickly outpaced reason.

Internet trading during the dot-com boom soon resembled trading frenzies from other eras. Radio was the technology that sparked the '20s stock boom. Like the Internet, it was a new medium with seemingly infinite possibilities. But the Internet boom may most closely resembled a much earlier period of obsessive trading, the South Sea Bubble of the early 1700s. Traders fed on the notion of wealth to be had from South America, a land few had even seen, but which they understood to be larger than Europe, and as yet almost totally undeveloped.

Only the Internet, located within the realm of cyberspace, could by its very nature be larger than any continent or world. It was infinite, and it was sure to be an engine of infinite wealth. Therefore, so it was argued, the old rules of value, price, and reason should not be applied to Internet investing.

Of course, this was wrong. But it didn't stop day traders from riding up the prices of Internet stocks. Some made millions in the process and were smart enough to see that an end to the good times would inevitably come. Others continued to believe, and they watched their profits dissolve into the ether of cyberspace. There are examples of both in this book.

Day trading all but ended with the dot-com bust, both as a captivating movement and as a way to make a fortune. But over the years, the markets stabilized, the tools improved, and a new more adept generation of day traders slowly emerged.

This new breed of traders is wise to the mistakes and successes of their earlier peers. Anyone who wishes to join their ranks would be well advised to do the same.

2010

Acknowledgements

Many people helped make this book possible. I would like to especially thank the 12 traders whose stories appear here. Each gave generously of their time during lengthy and at times gruelling interviews. Equally important, each shared his or her invaluable insights into the trading life, including coveted techniques, and even some lesson-filled mistakes, all in the interests of helping other traders succeed. Special thanks also to David Richardson and Andrew Vallas at Prima Publishing, for their faith in me throughout this project. My warmest thanks go out to Steve Harris, publisher of *Online Investor* magazine and to Jan Parr, the magazine's editor, along with the rest of her staff. Early in 1998, Jan telephoned me to say she was in charge of launching a new magazine, one aimed at helping self-directed investors make best use of the Internet. Would I be interested in becoming one of her contributors, she wanted to know? I remember that day distinctly because it was the beginning of a fascinating new direction for my own writing: covering the incredible boom in online trading. That boom continues, even as markets surge and decline. All the while, Jan's help and encouragement have been immeasurably helpful, as the articles all of us involved with the magazine worked on tried to explain how the Internet was empowering investors and traders as never before. Later I would be grateful to receive a similar invitation from Jamie Heller and David Landis at TheStreet.com to cover online trading for that financial Web site. The knowledge I've gained by researching articles for *Online Investor* and writing columns for TheStreet.com has been an enormous help in producing this book. Both organizations have allowed me to be a part of one of the most exciting developments at the turn of the century. And for that, I will always be thankful.

Chapter One
Introduction: Renegades in Cyberspace

Can day trading make you a millionaire? No way, says a June 12, 2000, article in *Forbes* magazine. The article cites a study by the former North American Securities Dealers Association (NASD, the administrative and regulatory arm behind the NASDAQ stock exchange*), which found that 77 percent of day traders in fact lose money. The average profit over the course of eight months was a paltry $22,000, the study revealed, or a little more than you'd earn if you were an especially annoying telemarketer. In all, the NASD survey scrutinized the accounts of 124 day traders. It found only two cases in which traders earned $100,000 or more. That's less than a mediocre stockbroker makes on commissions, the *Forbes* article noted. The implied message, seemingly: It's better to steer clients into bum trades than to make those bum trades using your own money.

Pay a visit to the Securities and Exchange Commission's (SEC) Web site and you find more dire warnings about day trading. "Be prepared to suffer severe financial losses", a headline on the site warns. Beneath the headline, the text reads, "Day traders typically suffer severe financial losses in their first months of trading, and many never graduate to profit-making status." Moreover, the SEC notes that "day trading is an extremely stressful and expensive full-time job."

A TV commercial for Barclays Bank that's aired frequently on CNBC reinforces the idea that day traders are in deep denial when they think they can make a living by trading their own accounts. The ad depicts an unwashed, unshaven, and slightly unhinged trader at work in his pajamas. We watch as he racks up profits of $16 or $64, even while his life savings stand in danger of evaporating at any moment.

---

*In 2007, the NASD merged with the New York Stock Exchange's regulatory body and changed its name to the Financial Industry Regulatory Authority (FINRA

Success stories

Happily, the traders profiled in this book belie that stereotype. And for that reason alone, we can learn a lot from their stories and the strategies they've used to succeed. Their record of success is vastly better than the findings of the NASD survey. To secure a place in this book, each trader had to build an account that totalled seven figures or higher. Alternately, over the course of their careers they needed to have taken at least seven figures from the market. The great majority of the 12 traders did far better than that. Some succeeded in earning more than $1 million. One trader, Mary Pugh, in keeping with the book's subtitle, did sustain losses well in excess of $1 million. But prior to that, she had built her account up by many millions more. And her losses occurred mainly because she chose to place a major portion of her portfolio in a small, highly speculative tech firm.

Far more common were losses of hundreds of thousands of dollars incurred during the tech wreck of spring 2000. But even when factoring in these huge losses, the traders were still left with accounts that were vastly higher than the sums they began with. Their returns of 100 percent to as much as 1,000 percent or more would impress even the most out-on-the-edge hedge fund manager.

The stories of how these traders amassed that money are indeed true tales of guts and glory. Teresa Lo let close to $1 million ride on long index options – one of the most risky trading arenas you'll find. Over the weeks her profits grew. But she refused to take the funds off the table, even though she knew an unexpected market downturn might render her entire options portfolio worthless. Terry Bruce grew his portfolio from $75,000 to well over half a million in just six months, only to watch it crash back to zero following a series of bad trades. To get back into the trading game, he took out a second mortgage on his house. The $40,000 he amassed would serve as both trading capital and expense money. And he knew if he lost it, he'd find himself practically out on the street. During the turbulent markets that occurred during late '99 and into 2000, Barbara Hamilton found herself making and losing as much as $100,000 in the course of a single day!

A new breed of entrepreneur

The stories these traders have to tell are all the more remarkable when you consider that many came from very different walks of life before taking up trading. True enough Lo, Oliver Velez, Brendan DeLamielleure, and Chris Farrell served stints with brokerage houses before they began trading their own accounts full-time. But they are the exceptions. Before taking up trading, Barbara Hamilton was a classical pianist and then a software programmer, Mary Pugh worked for top-level New York ad agencies. Terry Bruce made a good living as a photographer. Over time, like civilians drafted into the Army, they became hardened market veterans. And their performance, as you'll see, often exceeded that of Wall Street's best money managers.

Indeed, a decade or so ago, before the advent of the Internet and the spread of deep discount online brokerages, these same people might have sought their fortune by starting their own companies. Or, they might have reached for brass rings in the entertainment industry, maybe by writing a screenplay, or waiting tables while they auditioned for acting jobs. In all likelihood, trading offers a better chance at success than any of these alternatives. Only a handful of aspiring screenwriters and entertainers ever achieve true success. Likewise, if you start a small business – even a boring business like a yogurt stand or a quick lube shop – your odds of success are pretty dismal. Roughly nine out of ten businesses fail in their first years of existence, according to the U.S. Small Business Administration. The successful ones hemorrhage money for years before turning a profit. And during those manic early years, small-business owners must continually scramble to find cash to pay their suppliers and employees. Besides worrying about the product and customers, small-business owners tear their hair out dealing with regulations, personnel flare-ups, irate landlords, and a plethora of other problems.

Why day trading is so appealing

Trading for a living seems elegantly simple by comparison. Moreover, it's the sort of career or second career that you can begin immediately. First, learn all you can about investing. Read books. Tune into Web sites like Finance Yahoo, TheStreet.com, Quicken.com, and CBS MarketWatch. Listen to CNBC in the morning while you take a shower. Set up a personal computer with a fast Internet connection. And finally, open an online account with $50,000. And you're set to go. As one successful trader (not profiled in this book) told me, "This is the one thing that I can do where I feel like I have control over everything. I don't have any employees. I don't have to worry about suppliers." Seated at his computer, he, like other traders regularly matches wits with Wall Street's best and brightest. And quite often he wins.

To be sure, becoming a successful trader can take months or even years. And some people simply aren't cut out for the job. For those entirely new to the subject, the appendix contains a primer on trading. But for now let's focus on that $50K in start-up capital, the minimum amount most trading coaches say you need to get started. It's the Information Age equivalent of a stake in a poker game.

> **Call day trading the new American Dream. Its allure is especially strong for those who've served time in unfulfilling jobs, those who've been downsized, underemployed, or otherwise left out of the '90s economic boom.**

But in today's economy, it's not really that much money. Fifty thousand dollars wouldn't buy you very much of a business, for example. And without a separate source of income, such as a spouse's salary, you'd be hard pressed to pay your business expenses and your living expenses in the early months.

Therein lies the allure of day trading: It's an opportunity to turn a modest sum into a fortune, and in a short time. "If you're good at it," notes Brendan DeLamielleure, "there's not a higher margin business in the world." Call day trading the new American Dream. Its allure is especially strong for those who've served time in unfulfilling jobs, those who've been downsized, underemployed, or otherwise left out of the '90s economic boom. When you launch your trading career, there's no need to worry about finding investors, as would be the case with a brick-and-mortar business. No need to worry about customers beating a path to your door. There are stories of really daring traders – and also fool-hardy. I'd hasten to add – who have amassed their $50K stake by maxing out their credit cards. As long as the potential exists for people to make so much money by putting together a comparatively small stake, day traders will remain with us. Sure lots will flame out and go back to crummy day jobs, just as most people who start small businesses fail and most aspiring actresses fail and most novelists. But a long line of newcomers will always be there, ready to take their places.

That is as long as the potential exists to make money in the markets. To make money, all traders really need is volatility. Needless to say, over the last several years the markets have been notably obliging in that regard.

Unique strategies

Which brings up how the traders profiled in this book can be especially helpful to anyone who's thought about joining their ranks. Each of the 12 traders you'll read about has developed a unique strategy. You could think of this book as a kind of sampler of artistic styles. And – yes – the most successful traders play the market the way a skilled musician plays an instrument.

One trader, Bob Martin, who's a lawyer from Wichita, Kansas, looks for successful, fast-growing companies called "gorillas" with knockout technology. He either takes positions in a highly diversified basket of these companies and waits for them to grow, or else he uses the shares he owns to execute an options strategy known as "covered call writing." Chris Farrell searches out extremely stable stocks that trade on the New York Stock Exchange (NYSE). One could truthfully call them boring stocks. But Farrell likes them that way. He earns a living $\frac{1}{16}$ of a point at a time by getting inside the bid and ask spread. And as you'll see, his strategy takes advantage of a couple of unique rules governing trading on the NYSE. Another trader, Barbara Simon, a former graphic artist, has made herself an expert on how stocks trade in the days

" As long as the potential exists for people to make so much money by putting together a comparatively small stake, day traders will remain with us. Sure lots will flame out and go back to crummy day jobs, just as most people who start small businesses fail and most aspiring actresses fail and most novelists. But a long line of newcomers will always be there, ready to take their places. "

immediately before and after they announce their quarterly earnings. Brendan DeLamielleure watches 5-minute tick charts. Like a violinist watching a conductor's baton, he waits for the precise moment when he should play a stock or withdraw. And then there's Scott McCormick, who's worked on classified engineering projects for the Defense Department. Each night he searches for market opportunities by running a list of stocks through an artificial intelligence software program he's devised.

Some of the traders put relatively small amounts of money into play. Others bet the farm on expensive, highly volatile stocks. Some hold certain positions for months, even years. Others might jump in and out of a stock in a matter of seconds.

Who's a day trader?

Are they all, in fact, day traders? Probably not, at least in the strictest sense. By most definitions, a day trader is a person who buys and sells stocks over the course of day. Just before the markets close, except in rare instances, day traders sell off everything they own and revert their accounts to cash – the better to sleep at night, since market-wrenching events can occur at any time around the world.

This book utilizes a somewhat broader definition of day trading. A day trader, for the purposes of this book, is someone who closely follows the market each and every day. All of the 12 traders fit this profile. For several hours each day you'll find them in front of their monitors. (Some watch as many as eight monitors!). A few track the markets from the moment they wake up until the moment they fall asleep, still holding a chart or the latest research report on some high-flying company. In fact, nearly all the traders I spoke with claim they lose their edge when they stay away from the markets for too long. Nevertheless, several traders do manage to hold down demanding day jobs and still make good money in the markets. Their examples prove you don't have to quit your day job and withdraw from the world to become a successful day trader. And they can teach newcomers plenty about how these individuals juggle the demands of family and jobs with trading.

Methodology

And that brings up a key question: Are the results claimed by the traders in this book consistent with what an average trader might achieve? Are these traders unique, in other words? Granted, locating the 12 traders wasn't done using anything like a scientific search. Most came to me through referrals from colleagues whose help I am grateful for. But it's worth noting that finding traders who'd make $1 million or more wasn't especially difficult. Before settling on the list here, I amassed a much lengthier pool of candidates.

I should mention a couple of additional points concerning the methodology used to complete this book. Once a trader agreed to be included, the actual interview took place by phone. In all cases, I relied on the traders themselves to supply the details of their trading history. In no case were their accounts audited. In several instances, traders felt uncomfortable naming specific amounts of money. When that happened, I referred to things like the value of their portfolio in broad terms. Also, two of the traders (they're noted in the relevant chapters) requested that their real names not be used. In those instances, I recreated pseudonyms and changed other personal details, out of respect for their privacy.

But again the question: Is this a representational group? My answer to that would be No and Yes. No, because all likely would be regarded as successful in whatever area they chose to focus their energies. Oliver Velez manages several companies that are outgrowths of his success as a trader. Five other traders in the book manage Web sites where they advise other traders. And their subscribers pay anywhere from $25 to $250 per month for the privilege of receiving their advise in real time. Then there are those who juggle demanding jobs. Bob Martin – the covered call writer – is a trial lawyer representing companies in product liability cases. Scott McCormick – the designer of AI trading software – is a top-level manager at a tech firm. In other words, they and several others in the book prove they can succeed at business as well as the markets. And in that sense they are exceptional people.

It also must be said that the time period during which this book was written was an exceptional one for the markets. Throughout the latter half of the '90s, NASDAQ tech stocks in particular rose to unimaginable heights. That record breaking bull run went parabolic during the fall of '99 and continued into the early months of 2000. And indeed, it was in January and February 2000 that many of the 12 traders saw their accounts top the $1 million mark.

Then, of course, came one of the steepest corrections in recent memory. The best – or maybe it's the luckiest – traders were those who somehow saw the crash coming and were able to preserve their capital. What led them to correctly predict that the sky was falling and how they reacted during the scary days of March and April 2000 can hold some valuable lessons for any trader or investor, as markets have continued on a choppy course ever since.

❝ They are the kind of regular people you might run into at the supermarket or dry cleaners. Yet by they own volition they have entered a world where each day, when they turn on the computer, they put their entire net worth on the line. ❞

Renegades rule

To be sure, during that period many of the other 12 suddenly found their accounts diminished by hundreds of thousands of dollars. (Others quickly adapted and have since seen their accounts grow to new heights.) To put those heavy losses into perspective, it's worth reflecting again on who these traders are. Whether extraordinary in their abilities or not, they are the kind of regular people you might run into at the supermarket or dry cleaners. Yet by they own volition they have entered a world where each day, when they turn on the computer, they put their entire net worth on the line. Moreover, each day their potential gains and losses sometimes far exceeded what most Americans might earn in a year's time. In the course of buying and selling each day, they moved millions through the markets.

"Moving money from stock to stock, wagering their skills in daily battles against the very best of Wall Street, that tremendous sea of capital put in play by day traders has challenged the market's most powerful players. "

Yes, it's true: Had the bull market not come about, many might not have taken to trading at all. But because these 12 traders and thousands like them have taken to trading, they've managed to change the equity markets forever. By some estimates, active trades account for half of all trades made each day. Moving money from stock to stock, wagering their skills in daily battles against the very best of Wall Street, that tremendous sea of capital put in play by day traders has challenged the market's most powerful players – namely the market makers, the institutions, the hedge funds, and the brokerage houses.

What's not commonly known outside of Wall Street circles is that all of the traditional power players – the hedge funds, the institutions and so on – themselves employ traders who buy and sell on behalf of their firms. And those traders employ many of the same basic tactics used by the 12 traders you'll read about in this book. Over the decades, those tactics have yielded billions of dollars for their firms. Why then should it seem so incredible that individual traders using essentially the same tools can achieve the same results?

In the coming chapters you'll learn much about this new kind of investor and how they adapt their strategies to face markets that appear to grow ever more turbulent. Precisely how they've come to feel at home in the brave new world they've helped create is perhaps the most valuable lesson of all that they can teach us.

A word about decimalization

The major exchanges were beginning the apparently arduous task of converting to decimalization just as this book was going to press. For that reason many of the stock quotes you see here are depicted using fractions. That might make them seem quaint by the time you read this. Nevertheless, I don't think I'm being old-fashioned or curmudgeonly when I say I'm having a hard time quickly adding figures with four decimal places in my head. We may all wish for a return to fractions.

Chapter Two
How to Grow $20,000 into $1,000,000 in One 'Horrible' Year
Teresa Lo: The Intelligent Speculator

After all the wildness and chaos of 1996, Teresa Lo now strictly limits herself to day trading. Which was not a bad decision at all, the way she sees it. Because she "goes flat" each night – that is, she closes out all of her positions and reverts to cash – Lo says she's a lot more relaxed these days. And she has more time to spend with her husband and daughter, and on hobbies such as gourmet cooking. On weekends she and her family will treat themselves to a dim sum brunch. And it's then that she's able to forget about the market entirely.

In fact, by any accounts Lo would be considered an excellent day trader, even though she's not trading as frenetically as before. Years of experience have taught her to work the market with the precision of a neurosurgeon. Lo trades S&P e-minis, which are one-fifth the size of standard futures contracts written on the Standard and Poors 500 Index. She will buy and sell maybe five e-minis at a time, going long or short, depending on what the charts tell her. She rarely holds a position for more than 15 minutes. Her trades are mainly a means of instructing others in the chat threads she leads The Intelligent Speculator (www.ispeculator.com).

Trading on irrational exuberance

And she should know. Because the methodical, conservative – she'll even call it boring – style of day trading Lo uses today is eons removed from the mind-numbing gambles she took when she was in her late twenties and early thirties. That was when she traded heavily in markets as diverse and esoteric as

Canadian penny gold mining stocks and Nikkei Index options. Then, as now, Lo's trading style was built on the theory that markets often behave irrationally. They skyrocket up, and then they crash and burn. And if you jump in at the right time – as Lo has succeeded in doing – you can make a million or more in just months. The trick, of course, is knowing when to get out.

Lo witnessed these kinds of manic market gyrations for nearly 20 years, when she was growing up in Vancouver, British Columbia, a city famous for its penny gold stock exchange. During that time, the world economy also was in one of its more unruly periods. In the '70s and '80s, high interest rates, speculative frenzies, and shortages of basic items like gasoline and sugar created regular boom and bust cycles.

"Ever since I was a kid," Lo says, "I remember these weird things about people. I'd stand there and watch moms wait in line for sugar and gas. During the real estate boom, you'd make somebody an offer on a house, and then the piece of paper with the offer written on it would trade hands four or five times."

Gold, too, was routinely traded as a speculative commodity. Lo remembers seeing people lined up before the banks opened in order to buy gold. Her own father was at times an avid gold trader. "Every day when the quote came through, everybody had to be quiet," Lo recalls.

Indeed, her father, a career military officer, lost money when the markets for both gold and real estate crashed. The memories of those wild market gyrations stayed with her. "I found it so curious that everyone was so preoccupied with buying gold, real estate, whatever," she says. "Now, when we look back, we can see that all of those things were parabolic bubbles, where the prices just moved in a trajectory that was completely unsustainable."

To find more examples of parabolic bubbles, you need only follow the many penny gold stocks that trade on the Vancouver Stock Exchange. "With penny gold stocks," Lo explains, "when there's a new gold discovery the price will rise from 20 cents to $3 per share. That's a lot of money. But if you look at a chart and how it moves in terms of the trajectory, it's no different than what happened to Iomega or Qualcomm more recently."

Black Monday: the view from inside

In 1987, Lo, who was then in her early twenties, took those lessons with her when she went to work as an assistant broker for Canaccord, Canada's largest independent investment firm. The job gave her a unique insider's view of the markets. And she quickly saw how astute insiders could leverage their knowledge to trade their own accounts profitably. It was an invaluable insight. Because she was fresh out of college herself, Lo had very little in the way of savings. But as an employee of the firm, that was hardly a problem. Brokers at Canaccord could trade commission-free. Not only that, they didn't need a fully funded account. Canaccord permitted its employees to trade on generous margins. That is, the firm in effect advanced its employees much of the money they used to buy and sell stocks.

The market is not a machine, as those who search for the ultimate trading system or indicator believe. Rather, the market is made up of people who act on hopes and fears, whose motivations come from the dark recesses of the mind.

It's a system that is common at many brokerages in the United States as well. The margin requirements some brokerages charge their own employees can be as low as 20 percent. "Basically, it was acknowledged that as a broker you weren't paid any reasonable salary," says Lo. So these trading privileges were regarded as a perk. As long as traders could reconcile their accounts within the allotted number of days, they could use the powerful leverage the firm gave them to rack up huge gains. Indeed, Lo saw that the firm's best trader commonly realized annual trading profits of six figures or more.

Trading on margin is rarely a problem for those who go long in a strongly uptrending market. And the markets in the United States and Canada were steaming throughout much of 1987. Lo began trading in April of that year, focusing mainly on the Vancouver-traded penny gold stocks. In that era, long before Internet trading and the advent of CNBC, Lo's job at Canaccord provided her with a literal window on the market that was unavailable to those outside the business. Inside Canaccord's office was a black-and-white TV monitor that provided a live view of the Vancouver Exchange floor. Lo discovered that she could often gauge near-term market sentiment just by watching the expressions on the faces of the floor traders. In true contrarian fashion, whenever she sensed that panic on the floor was universal, it was a signal that a turnaround was imminent.

However, in the spring and summer of '87, most traders were caught up in the buying melee, and panic was far from their minds. Penny gold stocks doubled and quadrupled within a single trading day. Stocks of obscure British

Columbian mining ventures that sold for 20 cents on Monday might climb to $5 by Friday. Lo built up her profits by quickly flipping in and out of positions.

By early fall that year, Lo and other traders at her firm were beginning to suspect that a top had been reached. And many gradually cut back on their long positions. "I noticed in about August that it became really hard to make money, because things were just churning," she says. "So I didn't try. By some grace of God I stopped trading."

> **"The mind-sets of a professional trader and an amateur trader are often totally different. Pit a professional against an amateur, and the professional will likely win every time. "**

But when Black Monday arrived on October 19, 1987, Lo and the firm's other traders saw a once-in-a-lifetime opportunity. As the market crumbled before their eyes, "one of the floor traders came by with a list of what were thought to be the most highly margined stocks on the Vancouver Exchange." Lo recalls the man telling everyone, "This list is going to be hit by waves and waves of margin calls. Any uptick, just sell it short."

"So we went to work," says Lo. "The week after the crash was horrible ... just rounds and rounds of liquidations. And most of those things never came back."

The Black Monday incident helped Lo realize that she'd been wise to learn how to trade by working as a broker inside a firm. The mind-sets of a professional trader and an amateur trader are often totally different. Pit a professional against an amateur, and the professional will likely win every time. In one of a collection of essays you'll find on her Web site, she writes:

> A professional trader probably began studying the market and its psychology at a relatively young age and gained employment in the stock brokerage business in order to make contacts and to develop the skills required to consistently make trading profits ... A retail trader is typically a person with a real job, someone who saved up to take a punt on hope that Lady Luck might parlay the spare cash into a tidy sum.

> The difference between the future professional trader and the punter is apparent at the beginning of the long journey. One believes that trading is a learned skill based on the disciplined application of knowledge, risk, and money management. The other believes the market is a gamble, so what the hell, and comes to play with whatever he or she can afford to lose. In the game as we know it, the pros are few and the punters are many. Given the attitude, no wonder the market is viewed by the majority as a lottery.

Pyramiding to ruination

Lo herself was determined not to be a punter. Nevertheless, like all traders, she made her share of mistakes early on. One of those mistakes occurred roughly a year after the Black Monday massacre. Lo had begun trading gold stocks once again. To boost her profits she tried a common investment technique called "pyramiding." Traders using pyramiding increase the size of a position that's moving in their favour. So, for example, if you bought 100 shares of IBM at 104 and the stock subsequently moved to 108, you might add another 50 shares if you believed the stock was likely to continue rising.

Pyramiding works especially well during sustained bull markets – where you are adding to a long position. Adding to a short position during a sustained bear market is more difficult and far riskier, since the false rallies that are common to bear markets can be steep enough to trigger margin calls.

But with bull markets the technique can nicely augment your gains. Nevertheless, most trading experts advise you to add progressively smaller and smaller amounts to your position – hence the term pyramiding. Your initial position is the largest, forming the base of the pyramid, while any successive amounts are gradually less and less. In that way, each new buy entails successively less risk.

Pyramiding gets dangerous when you add equal amounts to a position – as many traders intent on riding a bull market are tempted to do. It's all the more dangerous if you're doing it on margin, as Lo discovered. "If you start with one position, and you double it and double it again, the average price you paid for all those shares very quickly moves up to very close to the market. So just a small setback can totally wipe you out."

> **" Pyramiding gets dangerous when you add equal amounts to a position – as many traders intent on riding a bull market are tempted to do. It's all the more dangerous if you're doing it on margin, as Lo discovered. "**

When Lo's gold stocks pulled back, she was hugely over-leveraged. She counts herself as lucky that she was able to get out with just a $20,000 loss. "Certainly," she says in retrospect, "if you buy 1,000 shares and you want to buy more on a pullback, don't buy another 1,000. Buy 300. So your average cost is far behind whatever the average price is now. That way if it bounces or dips you can still get out with a small profit.

Twice burned

A year later, when gold stocks were again on a tear, Lo failed to take her own advice. This time the losses totaled $100,000, effectively wiping out her trading account. Once again, she considers herself lucky that she didn't owe the firm any money. But as a trader she was dead in the water.

So Lo went into crisis mode. "I figured, 'I'm not going to let this thing win.'" For six months she worked three jobs: in the mornings, as a broker at Canaccord, which kept her busy until the markets closed on the east coast, which was 1:30 Pacific Time. During the afternoons, she handled the paperwork on the day's orders from Canaccord's customers. At the same time she worked as a mortgage broker. Her pager would sound whenever someone needed information on a loan. Then from 6:30 to 11 most evenings she put together take-out orders at a Tony Roma's restaurant.

The whole ordeal, she says, ended up having a four-fold effect: "First of all, it was good punishment for the sins that I had committed in my mind. The three jobs actually did pay some pretty good money. Third, I couldn't go out any more, so I couldn't spend anything. And Tony Roma's was feeding me ribs every night."

After many months, Lo amassed a stake of $50,000, enough to get her back into the game. Just as important, she felt confident once again. "If you don't know what you did wrong and you lose all your money, then you have a huge problem. I had made all that money in the market once before. I figured, if I just don't make the same mistakes, with some capital, I should be able to make that money back."

Thus, pyramiding was permanently removed from her trading repertoire. The ordeal also helped Lo further refine her trading strategy. She vowed she'd tune out all the market noise that had clouded her decisions before and hone in on the basics. "The price and the volume never lie," she said. "And you better just believe what's on your screen."

Riding the wild Nikkei

Instead of gold stocks, this time Lo chose an even more exotic instrument: options on Japan's Nikkei stock index. Options of any sort are difficult for many beginning investors to understand. And to really learn about them you should read a book such as *Getting Started in Options* by Michael C. Thomsett.

Most people are even less familiar with index options. Very few active traders ever dabble in the ones written on U.S. stock indexes like the Dow or the NASDAQ. Even fewer trade options on foreign stock indexes such as the Nikkei.

For that reason, options require a brief explanation. Options come in two varieties: calls and puts. A call gives you the right to buy a security at a certain price, called the "strike price." What's more, you can exercise that right at any time before the option's expiration dated. A put is just the opposite of a call. It gives you the right to sell a security at a predetermined strike price at any point between the time you buy it and the put option's expiration date.

If all this sounds complicated, there's an easy way to remember it: If you're bullish on a stock buy a call; if you're bearish, buy a put. Conversely, if you think a stock is going down, you might sell a call. And if you think it's going up, you might sell a put.

Unlike stocks, which will likely always maintain some value, options become totally worthless if a trader fails to exercise them before the expiration date. If you buy options, any losses you sustain will be limited to whatever price you paid for the option in the first place. However, if you sell options, your losses can be devastating. If the stock rises past the strike price of the call you've sold, you're still obligated to hand over that stock at the strike price called for by the option contract. That means you may have to buy those shares at their current market price and then turn them over to your broker, who will settle the option for you. Conversely, if you sell a put option at a strike price of $50 and the stock drops to $10 per share, you're still obligated to purchase those shares for $50.

Options on foreign stock indexes are an order of magnitude more complicated. For starters, most trade on the Philadelphia Stock Exchange, a market few people outside the trading profession and outside of Philadelphia have even heard of. The mechanics of index options differ slightly from equity options, too. In certain instances, an index option gives you the right to acquire the entire basket of shares making up a particular index, such as the S&P or the Nikkei. However, in practice people simply sell the options – either at a gain or a loss – before they expire.

Why do people trade foreign index options? One reason: Institutional investors may use index options as a hedge against their foreign stockholdings. For example, if you're a mutual fund manager with heavy holdings in the Japanese stock market, you might purchase some puts as insurance in case the Japanese stocks in your portfolio crash. Since puts give you the right to sell stock at a specific price, any downward move in the Nikkei Index would result in the put increasing in value. In this way, gains made on the eventual sale of the puts would help offset any losses in the stocks you won. Of course, if the Nikkei were to surge upward, the puts would decline in value until eventually they expired worthless. But remember, you purchased these puts as a kind of insurance policy. If the puts expired worthless, it means that your portfolio as a whole would have grown in value thanks to the increasing price of its component stocks. For prudent investors this is a win-win strategy if executed properly.

By contrast, for individual speculators such as Teresa Lo, index options offer the prospect of fantastic gains or crushing losses. Both result from the huge leverage they offer.

From February to March 1993, that leverage seemed all the more enticing. The Nikkei had bottomed out. And Japan was wallowing in a recession that would last the remainder of the decade and beyond. With such a bleak economic forecast, no one expected a significant move in the Nikkei anytime soon. Therefore, call options on the Nikkei Index with strike prices well above the index's current level were selling for practically nothing.

At the same time, Lo and other traders at Canaccord noticed that the charts tracking the Nikkei had seemingly bottomed out. "It was a major low," she recalls. "All of the cycles were coming together on the daily, weekly, and monthly charts. One of the guys in the office said, "We've got to take a punt on this."

Soon a small group of traders at Canaccord began buying calls with expiration dates from one to two months out. "We weren't being very scientific," Lo recalls. "We'd buy some for a month out and buy some for a couple of months out. We did it very slowly, because no one else was trading Nikkei calls at the time. And there was very little liquidity. We'd buy five each day, and we'd buy all kinds of different strikes so no one would figure out that it was us accumulating."

Lo herself eventually amassed roughly 100 Nikkei calls. Some were selling for as little as $5/16$ or $1. Which means she was paying $100 or less for the entire contract. All in all, she figures she wagered $15,000. That's a huge bet when you consider that the options she'd purchased were highly illiquid, and that their strike prices were 100 to 200 points above where the Nikkei currently languished. The odds were that Lo's options would simply expire worthless.

"Then one day I came into the office and there was a standing ovation," she remembers. "People said the Nikkei was up 600 points. Some of the calls went from $\frac{5}{16}$ to $15 or more." As a result of the sudden and unexpected rise in the Nikkei, traders elsewhere around the globe who had shorted Japanese stocks now needed to cover their positions or face gruesome losses. The panicked short covering, of course, drove up the Nikkei Index further. Lo and her fellow traders held on to their positions as long as they dared before the option's expiration in order to catch as much of this price rise as possible. Her $15,000 bet had returned roughly $100,000.

The year of living dangerously

After her success trading Nikkei Index options, Lo took a break from trading in order to help care for her half-sister in California, who was gravely ill. Every other week she would hop a shuttle south from Vancouver to be with her. This went on for months, until her sister tragically died in December 1995.

It was then, on the flight home from the funeral, that Lo remembers going over some stock index charts. Again, the indicators all pointed to a major upswing. Only this time, the market was not options on a stock index located an ocean away. It was the rough-and-tumble Canadian gold stocks that traded on the Vancouver Exchange, her own backyard. To her the prices all seemed "washed out," despite the fact that gold during that period experienced occasional bear market rallies that offered the chance for substantial profits. Once again, in true contrarian fashion, Lo theorized that the near-dormant condition of gold stocks pointed to their imminent rise. Indeed, some stocks had already started creeping up.

Usually, Vancouver's penny gold stocks bottom out during November. This is the time when highly speculative mining companies begin soliciting funds for the upcoming season of exploration. It's not uncommon for shares that had sold for $2 just months before to sink to as little as 20 cents during this period. "They form a dish pattern on the charts while the volume shrinks," Lo says. "It's the really quiet bottoms that no one looks at that are the best."

This low volume occurs in part because retail traders normally steer clear of the market during the fund-raising period. But for professional traders like Lo, the late fall is seen as a good time to buy. Again these professional traders possess a distinct advantage over outsiders. Vancouver's trading community is relatively small. And most of its members are tied into the informal buzz being generated about prospecting companies at meeting rooms and bars around the city.

One of the spots these traders often frequented was a dingy, smoke-filled "peeler bar" or strip club located near Canaccord's office. No one was especially fond of the entertainment, Lo says. But the place was routinely jammed with traders because it often rained during this time of year, and it was the closest place where Canaccord's employees could find a drink. While the women danced on stage, the oblivious traders hunkered down and talked about gold.

What especially piqued their curiosity was the fact that options on the XAU – that is, the gold and silver index that trades on the Philadelphia stock exchange – had bounced handily off their previous lows. Moves of this sort occurred when stocks of the larger companies constituting the index experienced a rise. These stocks were considered bellwethers.

And the traders in the peeler bar believed this foreshadowed a rally. Lo and her colleagues knew that any rally in the larger mining stocks would be amplified as it spread to the more speculative penny stocks that traded on the Vancouver Exchange.

But which penny stocks? Here again, Lo was to benefit from the contacts she'd nurtured at Canaccord. One of those was John Kaiser, one of the leading analysts of speculative gold stocks. He is best known in the industry for his newsletter, the *Kaiser Bottom Fishing Report* (www.canspecresearch.com). In it Kaiser identifies the best bargains among speculative gold stocks. Lo examined Kaiser's recommendations carefully and ran them by John Muir, another highly regarded gold stock analyst. In cases where both men agreed, Lo bought about $2,000 worth of stock. Also, Lo based her decision on the prospecting venture's capitalization. Those that had received ample financing through private placements were normally companies that had done well in the past. Their current capitalization helped ensure they could continue to explore without going broke. "If one company hits something, then the rest of the companies will experience a stock run-up, too," she says. "So you really couldn't lose if you had a company with money, because that company could send guys out there by chopper to explore a nearby claim in just a couple of days."

Before she was through, Lo had invested about $20,000, spread among 10 companies. The winnowing process had taken about two weeks. Now it was time to wait.

Gold exploration can start as early as January. And this is a period when rumors, tips, and gossip can send the prices of 20-cent shares rocketing skyward. If one company makes a strike, and another company has an exploration license on a piece of real estate nearby, the stock of that second mining company will likely shoot up as well – something Lo calls "closeology."

As winter turned to spring, Lo watched her portfolio increase in value as momentum investors jumped in. When a stock looked overblown, she would sell it off in blocks. By late spring her $20,000 stake had mushroomed to $100,000. By this time, Lo was completely out of gold stocks. She decided to bet the entire 100,000 on something entirely different.

High anxiety and the S&P

This time the market Lo chose was options on the S&P 100 (OEX), which is the index of the 100 largest corporations that trade on North American exchanges. The options themselves trade on the Chicago Board Options Exchange (CBOE). Lo had definite reasons why she liked the market: This was a time on Wall Street when bigger was definitely better. Both U.S. and foreign investors all wanted a portfolio heavy on blue chips. "I think they were convinced that 'coke was it,' that it was going to be all magic."

Studying the charts, all the evidence suggested that this was a parabolic bubble in the making. "At the beginning of '96, during the second week of January, the low was 285 on the OEX," she says. "And it basically was up every week until February, when the high was 318. Then it chopped and chopped and chopped. And I remember telling everyone, 'This is one hell of a consolidation.' But what it looked like to me was a huge consolidation within a range. And it had held at the support levels that we had looked at before. There had been dips in March, which were scary. I think that was the first time the trading community started paying attention to unemployment numbers in a meaningful way. In April there was another dip. And another in May. But this time it made a higher low and it reversed on that day, and so I thought, 'Well, if that's the case, then it's going to go up sharply after consolidating for months.' I thought, 'This is it.'" In other words, after it had bounced around aimlessly, Lo believed the index had finally acquired some direction. "And it took off and I did it," she says.

Lo surmised that buying call options on the OEX would be the best way to ride any uptrend in the index. She and her colleagues at Canaccord had often traded OEX options in the past. Many experienced traders prefer options because of the high degree of leverage they afford. You may pay only $20 ($2,000) for a call option. That money theoretically controls a basket of stocks worth thousands more. And once the index is in the money, that is, once the underlying index reaches the strike price of the option, then any further increase in the price of the index will be matched roughly dollar for dollar by an increase in the option's price. Therein lies the opportunity for mind-boggling profits.

But losses can be crushing, too. Options are often referred to as "wasting assets." As noted earlier, their value declines as they approach their expiration date. Unlike stocks, which likely will decline only to the breakup value of a company, an option becomes utterly worthless once it expires. In theory, most options traders exit their long positions well before this happens. This is done simply by selling the call options they've purchased. But sudden market shifts can still wreak swift and terrible damage to an options portfolio. Lo was about to spend $100,000 on a wasting asset, the equivalent of a high-stakes bet at a baccarat table.

Her strategy remained fairly fluid. She bought the call options with strike prices more or less level with the OEX's current price, or "at the money," as this is called. The expiration normally would be 4-6 weeks from the date she purchased the option. The near-term expiration in particular minimized any time premium she'd have to pay. Alternately, by purchasing options at the money, she could exit a position without losing too great a percentage of the option's value.

Lo usually held on to her positions for a couple of weeks before selling. And she used daily charts to gauge where she thought the index was heading near-term in order to time her buys and sells effectively. "I used a 30-day moving average," she says. "Although I didn't really pay much attention to that either. I would watch TV and talk to the other traders at the firm."

" Sudden market shifts can still wreak swift and terrible damage to an options portfolio. Lo was about to spend $100,000 on a wasting asset, the equivalent of a high-stakes bet at a baccarat table. "

Even so, she says, "You never really knew what was going to happen. So long as the market was heading in the direction that I wanted, I would hold on to the option. If it had a couple of bad days, I would just get out." Her positions were highly concentrated, which meant that any move up or down would radically change her net worth. More cautious traders might have taken a portion of their gains and set them aside. But Lo saw this as her chance at a big-league score. And as the market rose, so did the amount she wagered. "I was trading ever-larger amounts," she says. "Because you had to hold these positions for days on end, every piece of economic news and data set me on edge. It was just horrible. I'd never endured anything like this in my life."

When the market corrected in July, Lo somehow managed to escape. She bought more options later on in July. Sold these soon after at a profit. And leaped back into the market in the fall, still betting ever-larger amounts. All the while she was aware that the July correction had planted seeds of doubt.

> **" More cautious traders might have taken a portion of their gains and set them aside. But Lo saw this as her chance at a big-league score. And as the market rose, so did the amount she wagered. "**

"This is what finally did me in, and why I don't trade very aggressively any more," she says. "July was the craziest month – the huge crash. And every month after that, it was going straight up. But it looked so tenuous. So it was terribly stressful. Between the July lows and the December highs, it would go up for a few days and then chop for a week."

Throughout the fall it was rare for Lo to get a good night's sleep. Everything she had learned as a trader told her that parabolic bubbles climb via a series of steep steps before reaching a top. Thus her trading account fluctuated by thousands each day as the market chopped. But as the market shot up, so did her net worth. And now it hovered precariously close to the seven-figure mark. Regardless, knowing when the final top arrives during a parabolic event is especially critical, since the fall-off that follows is far steeper than the long climb to the top. A fall-off could occur in a day. Any day.

Thinking back on it now, she vividly remembers Canaccord's annual Christmas party, held during the first week of December. "I wasn't drinking because I had to trade all the time," she says. "I became so obsessed with watching the market that I left the party two or three times to go upstairs. And I would watch the ticker, even though I couldn't trade overnight. The market would be down 20 points, and I thought, 'Oh my God.'"

All or nothing

For some reason, on New Year's Eve 1996, all the stress came to a head. "My sister was coming to visit," she remembers. "I had tickets for a New Year's Eve performance of the Three Tenors. I had bought tickets for my boyfriend, my mom, my sister and her boyfriend, and myself. They were $1,500 apiece. It had been a particularly horrible expiration the week before. And I was still wound up."

Lo remembers coming home to cook dinner. And then the taxi ride to the performance. As everyone settled into their seats at the concert, she spotted some of the people she worked at Canaccord. Suddenly the room began to spin. Her hands started to shake, and her heart pounded. She ended up having to leave before the concert even started.

That night and in the days that followed, Lo started coming to grips with all that had happened to her during 1996. The year had begun with the death of her half-sister and ended with Lo taking by far the biggest risk of her trading career. "It had been a whole year of doing really dangerous things, "she says. "I looked back and I thought, 'A year ago, when you came back from the funeral you had 20 grand, and look at this ... a million dollars.' And oh my God look at the risks I took to do it. What if it never worked out? I danced through a minefield for a whole year."

Ask her why she took such a huge risk, and why she didn't set a portion of her profits aside instead of letting the bet ride even as it grew progressively larger, and Lo will answer without hesitation. "Because to me, having 20 grand was the same as having nothing."

Daily rewards

Which doesn't mean the costs of that year haven't left their mark. Some months later, Lo left Canaccord and resolved to trade on her own. The idea for her Web site, The Intelligent Speculator, came about after she had sat in on several other online chat rooms. But for a variety of reasons she wound up not liking them. The Intelligent Speculator would be intended as a hangout for experienced traders like herself who were adept at reading trend lines and candlestick charts.

Indeed, after all the wildness and chaos that occurred in 1996, Teresa Lo now strictly limits herself to day trading. The S&P e-minis (or futures contracts) she now trades exclusively are similar to options in that they provide considerable leverage. Because S&P e-minis track an index, they tend to move continually in price. In fact, their short-term volatility is far greater than popular exchange-traded funds such as "Cubes" (QQQ), which track the NASDAQ 100. Because of this, Lo and her fellow traders at The Intelligent Speculator are able to exploit the contracts' volatility at numerous times during the day. Lo herself makes about three round-trip trades daily.

E-minis trade over a direct matching network called Globex2. This system, similar to electronic communications networks for stocks such as Island.com, provides enough liquidity for her to readily exit positions the instant the charts show that the market is moving against her.

Meanwhile, the bulk of her wealth is safely ensconced in T-bills. "People think day trading is glamorous and exciting. But it's really the last stop before you quit trading altogether. Usually you're so risk adverse that you only hold positions over 10 minutes or so. Once you've been in battle for so long and you've seen so many terrible things happen, you really don't want it to happen to you again."

Trading S&P e-minis online while she instructs both beginning and advanced traders, Lo has her methodology down to a science. "I use a 20-period exponential moving average (EMA) on the 15-minute chart," she says. "A lot of people use the 20-period EMA. So I just watch the bars because I know what they're going to do.

"I'm certainly a much better technical trader now than I've ever been. So I don't have to take big risks. There's only so much the human psyche can take," she says. "It's all relative. It's not whether you made millions or billions; it's how much money you started with and how many times you've multiplied that money. To someone like George Soros, a million-dollar bet is not that much. But to me $20,000 was all the money I had. By trading conservatively I don't have the same rewards. You never see those six-figure paydays. But you get paid every day. It'll just have to do because I can't take those risks again."

Teresa Lo's trading rules

- *Set realistic objectives.* If you're a trader you should really expect a minimum of 10 percent return on your capital every month. Or else you're doing something wrong. Gains larger than 10 percent are unsustainable over the long term.

- *Preserve your gains.* Consider removing the monthly profits you make from your trading account and investing those funds more conservatively.

- *Trade smaller positions on a longer time frame, versus large positions held for a short term.*

- *Only trade one thing at a time* (for example, stocks, futures, bonds or options). But trade them intensely. "There are very few people who have the talent to trade in more than one market at a time."

- *Trade speculative stocks with limited floats.* "As a former corporate financier, I knew that a great trick of the finance department is that if you limit the float, the stock can go up really fast. But it can also crash in about three seconds." Therefore any stock worth trading must be speculative. "Stocks with huge floats, such as Ford Motor Company, require huge amounts of buying and selling in order to experience meaningful price moves."

- *Buy on dips; sell (or short) temporary highs.* "If a stock has been rising in price for some time it's possibly in an uptrend. If it pulls back, buy it and monitor it closely. If it's still early in the uptrend, then it'll move up again. If the stock does move, and it touches the old high, you've encountered a point of resistance. If the stock doesn't blast right through the resistance point, exit your long position or consider selling the stock short.

- *Find a chart-reading method that presents simple indicators you can interpret easily.* "Chart reading in itself is very simple. There are only so many things that can be done with it, and all those fancy indicators are simply regurgitating the price with some math added to it."

- *Technicals work in the same way in every time frame.* But there are certain vehicles that are more noisy than others. For example, if you try to do candlesticks on a 5-minute Treasury bond chart, you're not going to get anywhere. Because it doesn't fluctuate enough to draw any meaningful candlesticks. So you have to move out to at least a 15-minute chart. A 5-minute chart will create a series of candlesticks that all look the same.

- *If you trade using candlestick charts, study the file intensely before acting on any of the more popular patterns.* "Candlesticks are great because they let you see what's happening from bar to bar. There's a real struggle between buyers and sellers. The less-well-known candlestick patterns are better. Everyone knows what a hammer and shooting star are." For that reason, these patterns can be dangerous. Beginners will see a hammer and decide to buy. And two bars later they're gone. You have to look for things like "piercing patterns" and "dark cloud covers" that most people don't really understand.

- *Don't be deluded into thinking you possess all the information about a stock, regardless of the quality of information about a stock, regardless of the quality of information appearing on your screen.* "The whole idea behind Level II is that by looking at who's trading what, you can figure out who's doing what. However, the institutional traders and the market makers and specialists are truly in a superior position. If they have something in their hand and they don't want to show you, I don't care what kind of claims the day trading firms make, you won't know."

- *Scalping is not cost effective.* "A lot of day trading academies say you can scalp for an eighth and be just like the market makers. I don't subscribe to that theory, because you have to risk a lot of capital to make very little money."

- *When buying options, large bets are necessary if you are to realize large gains.* However, all of your option positions should represent only a small portion of your portfolio. That way a miscalculation won't cause serious damage to your trading capital.

- *Only about 10 percent of the option positions you maintain should be locked into a single expiration date.*

- *Buy options that are at the money and within one or two weeks of expiration.* This minimizes the premium you pay for the option's time value. If your position moves against you by a couple of strikes, sell the option. Don't ride it to zero.

- *Trade the market as a scientist.* That is, you should observe and try not to affect the setting that you're observing. Be impartial and see what is really there instead of what you want to see.

Chapter Three
Trading Microtrends
Brendan DeLamielleure: The Tactician

A hot afternoon in early July, the market's been closed for just over half an hour, following another week of choppy, seemingly directionless trading. Sitting in the spare room of his St. Louis apartment, 28-year-old Brendan DeLamielleure (pronounced De-lama-lur) is not in a good mood. "Everything I get out of runs. Everything I stay in just comes right back where I bought it," he laments. "I took CAMP (California Amplifier, Inc.) as an overnight. I bought it after hours. I'm sitting on it all day and it's up 2 and some odd points. I step out a few minutes, and it's gone negative on just 10,000 shares volume!"

DeLamielleure's gripe was echoed by many traders who were trying to discern a direction from a directionless market during the summer of 2000. In laymen's terms, he's explaining that whenever he buys into a stock thinking it will rise, the stock hangs at its current price or-worse-retraces slightly. It's only after he sells the stock, cutting his losses, that the shares finally move up in price – another missed opportunity, another wrong guess. And if that's not bad enough, stocks DeLamielleure fails to sell retrace any gains they might have made while he owned them. And they tend to make sudden unexpected moves on light volume.

Either way, DeLamielleure's left with little to show when the trading day ends. "That's the problem with the market this summer," he says. "It's really nickel-and-dime crap. It's a very draining way to trade. You're not getting the same big moves in stocks."

Ironically, DeLamielleure's problem – getting in and out of stocks at precisely the wrong time – is similar to what many beginning investors face. Their fear prevents them from entering market rallies until they've just about reached their top. Consequently, the stocks they buy immediately decline in price. That same fear causes beginning investors to sell their positions when they reach bottom. In other words, they buy high and sell low. It's ironic that DeLamielleure himself should suffer from this problem, because he's hardly a beginner.

> **When no clear-cut long term trend emerges, traders have no recourse but to zoom in and look instead for – let's call them "microtrends" – that is, tiny movements in a stock's price that might play out over 5 minutes, or perhaps 15 minutes to an hour each day.**

Before setting out on his own in 1999, for three years he worked for a highly regarded St. Louis brokerage firm. During that time, he religiously developed trading tactics that he applied to his own trading. These tactics served him well during the market's parabolic rally of '99 as well as during the crash of spring 2000. DeLamielleure was able to take in an average of $2,500 per day, he says. In fact March 2000 proved to be DeLamielleure's best month, with April his second best. During March, while the market crashed all around him, DeLamielleure's trading account grew by $30,000. And incredibly (as will be explained later), he did it not by shorting stocks, but by going long. Beginning with a trading account of roughly $50,000, DeLamielleure traded his way to millionaire status by early 2000.

Unfortunately, DeLamielleure's trading style worked best when the market exhibited a clear-cut trend – either up or down. However markets only trend for brief periods. At all other times they merely wander. And when no clear-cut long term trend emerges, traders have no recourse but to zoom in and look instead for – let's call them "microtrends" – that is, tiny movements in a stock's price that might play out over 5 minutes, or perhaps 15 minutes to an hour each day. Indeed, that's what countless active traders were forced to do during the lacklustre low-volume trading days in summer 2000. Swing traders became day traders, and day traders become scalpers. Meanwhile, the market continued to outwit nearly all concerned.

The only thing that sucks about online trading is that if you're not there every day, you're not making a nickel. But if you're good at it, there's not a higher margin business in the world.

During that summer, DeLamielleure, while not a scalper, found himself trading more frenetically than he would have liked – sometimes 50 trades per day. "When I'm off I tend to make more trades. When I'm on I do under 15," he says. Those trades cost $15.95 each. As a result, DeLamielleure pays something like $200,000 per year in commissions. Enough to purchase an above–average home in most U.S. neighbourhoods. DeLamielleure shrugs off the expense. "I just don't think about it," he says. "It's a cost of doing business."

Trading school

Thanks to the fact that DeLamielleure apprenticed himself at his St. Louis firm for three years, he came to view all aspects of his trading as a business. That fact set him apart from countless people who take up day trading on a whim. Without the necessary skills and discipline, these newcomers often wash out after a few months. Like another trader profiled in this book, Teresa Lo (see page 11), DeLamielleure found his years of professional trading to be invaluable. "The advantage I think that I have over a lot of people is that I had a firm's capital at my disposal to learn how to trade before I went out on my own. I traded junk bonds," he says. "I also traded converts (convertible bonds). They move like molasses." Nevertheless, he says, "I made money for the firm. But my cut would be so small."

> **❝ DeLamielleure pays something like $200,000 per year in commissions. Enough to purchase an above–average home in most U.S. neighbourhoods. ❞**

Two years into his stint at the St. Louis firm, DeLamielleure and another trader who worked there resolved to try trading their own accounts. But being a careful, calculating sort, DeLamielleure decided a little practice was needed first. "I tried to determine what percentage of my trades were profitable, he says. "I sat right next to the NASDAQ traders, and so I put in trades for my own account, or I'd occasionally trade stocks for the firm."

At the same time, while he was under salary, DeLamielleure worked to amass his trading capital – which is to a trader what a stake is to a poker player. Many say that $25,000 is the bare minimum needed for a seat at the game. Trading on margin, that amount gives you control over $50,000, enough to buy 1,000 shares of a stock priced at $50 or less. Stocks in that price range might move by $1 or $2 on a given day. And that's the minimum volatility you need to produce a return you can live on. Still other experts advise beginners to pull together $50,000 before they begin. A higher stake is necessary to provide a cushion from the inevitable losses that will occur when you start. Lose your stake and you'll suddenly find yourself working as a telemarketer. If you go into active trading with too little money, these experts say, you'll sweat over each tiny move in a stock's price. This will cloud your judgment and eventually lead you to fail.

DeLamielleure figured he needed $50,000 to succeed. His wife worked as an engineer, so in a pinch she could support them. Making small trades while at the firm, DeLamielleure gradually built up his account. Then he saw an opportunity in Safeguard Scientifics (SFE), a Web incubator firm, similar to CMGI. Both Safeguard Scientifics and CMGI acted as holding companies for a family of fledgling Internet firms. At the time CMGI was a stock popular with traders of all kinds. Position traders and even buy-and-hold traditionalists liked the company because its diversified holdings offered a way to invest in the Internet sector through a single stock. That same diversification often caused CMGI stock to swing wildly on any news concerning the Internet sector. As a result, the stock was volatile enough to attract hell-flying momentum traders who regularly jumped in as the stock rode up and leaped off as it crashed downward. With so many traders playing CMGI, daily volume usually topped 5 million shares.

Thinking practically once again, DeLamielleure reasoned that he probably wouldn't get the chance to be first on board when a heavily traded stock such as CMGI began making an upward move. He was competing against more seasoned traders, for one. And many of those traders operated in trading rooms where they utilized lightning-fast-T1 connections to execute trades almost instantaneously. Moreover, CMGI was an expensive stock, trading back then at a split-adjusted $150 per share at times. With a price tag like that, DeLamielleure's trading capital didn't permit him to take a large enough position. And he was loath to buy it on margin.

However, second-tier stocks like SFE offered a plausible alternative. The company's market cap was roughly one-fourth CMGI's at the time. Average volume was under 1 million shares per day. And shares at the time traded in the more affordable under-$40 range. But most important, SFE stock tended to move in sympathy with CMGI's price. DeLamielleure figures that while he might not be first in line to exploit a price move by CMGI, he could beat the crowd and hop onto SFE at the first sign CMGI was about to make a run.

DeLamielleure put most of his stake into SFE and waited. "That was pretty much my make or break trade," he says. In all, he held on for six days. "I was pretty nervous. That was a good chunk of my money." But it returned a good chunk as well. About $30,000, enough for him to go out on his own.

Not only that, he'd found a winning strategy – chasing profits in second-tier stocks whenever the sector leader made a move. "If I see a stock that's moving in the wireless industry, I'm immediately on the hunt for anything else that's wireless," he explains. "I'll go to Yahoo! Finance (finance.yahoo.com) and get a profile of the company. I look at the float. I look at how much stock is outstanding. And I get a feel for how quick something will move," he says.

A level II world

DeLamielleure says the St Louis firm's managers, sensing that he might jump ship, offered him perks to stay. Those perks included low margin rates that would have greatly amplified the buying power of his 50K stake. "They offered us all kinds of deals if we were to stay," he says. Nevertheless, the SFE trade helped convince DeLamielleure he could make it on his own. Still, it was the kind of risk – putting the bulk of his capital into a single play – that he preferred not to take again. "If you don't do this as a profession, then it seems like you are a lot more ballsy," he reflects. "I was a lot more ballsy. Now I'm pretty much a wimp."

But a successful one. DeLamielleure's biggest profits were yet to come. But first he had to set up a trading room for himself. And that meant choosing the software he'd use to execute his trades. DeLamielleure opted for a program called Real Tick III (www.realtick.com) – which happened to be an easy choice, since it was the same trading platform he had used at the firm.

Execution platforms such as Real Tick III, which are used by serious traders, only vaguely resemble the order entry systems you see at the mainstream online brokerages where most of us maintain our accounts. Instead of a single screen where you type in your order, high-end trading platforms fill a computer monitor with as many as a dozen windows at once. One window might track broad market averages such as the Dow and NASDAQ. Another window might show a chart of a particular stock. On the bottom of the screen, a ticker scrolls by, showing real-time price changes on the list of stocks you want to monitor.

Still another window might display what are called Level II quotes for whatever stock you happen to be watching. Level II screens display only NASDAQ quotes.

Since the New York Stock Exchange (NYSE) uses a more centralized mechanism to execute trades (see chapter on Chris Farrell, page 79), its system for displaying quotes is far simpler. However, since most of the volatile technology stocks trade on the NASDAQ rather than the NYSE, active traders focus their attention there. Many of these traders build their strategies around the intricate and detailed information provided by a NASDAQ Level II screen. In fact, understanding a Level II screen's complexities can take weeks. But here's a brief explanation of how it works.

At the top of the Level II screen you see the best price currently available if you want to buy a stock. Right beside it sits the best price available for someone willing to buy that stock from you. The difference between those two prices is called the "spread". Below that best buy and best sell price you see a lengthy list of the buy and sell prices broadcast by other traders. These prices are fractionally off the current best price. The screen also lists the size of each offer, which may run the gamut from 100 shares to 10,000 or more. Some of these prices originate from the so-called market making firms – the exchange-sanctioned middlemen who buy and sell stocks in order to provide liquidity to the exchange. Other bids and offers originate from traders using electronic communications networks or ECNs. These are private trading systems that normally handle orders from individual day traders. In either case, the Level II screen displays the origin of the order, using a coded system of letters that traders soon memorize.

To make things more complicated, all the orders displayed on the screen continually change as traders field and rescind their bids in reaction to the moves made by their adversaries. The more heavily traded the stock, the faster the numbers change. Colors on the screen alert traders to price changes. And prices appear to move up and down the list as lower and higher bids and offers replace those that have been withdrawn. These changes often occur just milliseconds after the actual order is entered.

A skilled trader looking at the constantly changing numbers on the Level II screen tries to discern where the market is headed – and will be headed, often over the next several moments. Are there more sell offers than buy offers, for example? If so, then perhaps the price of the stock will move downward in the short run as supply exceeds demand. Are orders for large blocks of share suddenly appearing all over the screen? Perhaps that means a mutual fund or a hedge fund is anxious to acquire the stock – meaning the price might go up.

Hair-trigger trading

But appearances aren't always what they seem. Crafty traders – both the professional market makers and individuals – attempt to influence a stock's price by using their orders. For example, a trader might place an attractive offer to buy shares and then withdraw the order moments later. The idea is to draw sellers of the stock out of the woodwork. When the trader retracts the order he might replace it with a lower-priced offer to buy, hoping one or more the sellers will concede to meeting his price. These miniwars rage daily especially in the volatile technology and Internet stocks favored by active traders.

In order to stay alive, traders like DeLamielleure also need an execution window that's always at the ready on their computer monitors. This allows them to buy or sell a stock with a single keystroke or mouse click. Additionally, the execution window lets you target a particular bid displayed on the screen – one that might be slightly off the current best price. By targeting a bid you can execute a trade more or less directly with an individual offering to buy or sell stock at that price. This feature assists traders who want to move large positions quickly. And again, this can be done with a single keystroke or mouse click.

By contrast, the order entry screen used by most online brokerages requires that you confirm an order once it's placed. As an added safety measure, some online brokers require that you re-enter your password. To serious traders this means a loss of precious seconds. And in that short time span, the price of a stock can move past their target. Hence the need for turbo-charged software. To acquire that software active traders must sign on with a broker that caters to active traders. DeLamielleure opted for Terra Nova Trading (www.terranovatrading.com), which puts its own brand on the Real Tick platform. Other popular day-trading brokerages that have high-end execution platforms include CyBerCorp.com (www.cybercorp.com) And Tradecast.com. Some brokers charge as much as $300 per month for their software. The fees also cover the costs of receiving real-time price data from NASDAQ, the NYSE and other exchanges. But these fees are waived if you make, say, 50 or more trades per month. Each execution platform, whether from Real Tick or CyBerCorp.com, comes with a steep learning curve. And once they master the software, traders like DeLamielleure tend to stick with a system, even if this means – as in DeLamielleure's case – paying thousands of dollars in commissions each year.

"The biggest reason to stay with a broker is the opportunity cost," he says. "I can't really afford to have downtime while I figure out a new system. I might save $1,000 per month in commissions. But it could cost me $10,000 getting used to a new system."

DeLamielleure runs his software using two 19 inch monitors running off one computer. The monitors sit side by side so the effect is to create a single giant screen. On that ample landscape, he may place as many as three Level II screens. And he keeps a scrolling ticker so that he can monitor the 200 or so stocks he's most interested in.

A picture is worth a thousand bucks

But charts make up the most important element of DeLamielleure's screen. Specifically, they are 5-minute tick charts that track the aggregate moves made by traders during 5-minute periods – again, in real time. Looking at the way the charting program draws bars on the screen, it's possible to tell the price range that a stock has traded in during the period – from $30 ⅛ to $30 ⅜, for example. Just as important, a bar chart can tell you at what point buyers ceded control over the stock's price to sellers, and vice versa. In other words, an astute chart reader can quickly distill from a simple chart the confusing array of numbers displayed on the Level II screen. It's possible to draw similar bar charts using any time variable you like: 15 minutes, 30 minutes, 1 day, 1 month, whatever. But many day traders believe that a 5-minute chart gives the most readable picture of the microtrends that can emerge during the course of a single day's trading.

Like other successful traders, DeLamielleure took several years to learn the craft of chart reading. And during that time he made a daily habit of looking at charts of stocks he happened to be following. The result for DeLamielleure, as for other traders, is that the charts became second nature. "If you look at 100 tick charts every day for a couple of years, the patterns just come right at you," he says. And those patterns signal trading opportunities. "First of all, I look for erratic moves," he says. "If I see a stock just ticking along and all of a sudden there's a giant spike up and there's no news, I always short it. If there's a giant tick down, and there's no news, nine times out of ten I'll go long with the stock."

Trading strategies

Using charts as a starting point, DeLamielleure has devised a series of rules that govern his trading. "Entry points are the most important thing," he explains.

"A lot of times I buy stocks that are weak and trying to find a bottom. If the stock's coming down I use a long-term chart (15 minutes) to find a trend." That trend may indicate that the stock is moving lower in price over the course of the trading day.

If DeLamielleure believes the stock's decline is only temporary, he'll build a position via a technique known as "averaging down." Averaging down – also known as "doubling down" – is a common tactic used by both stock traders and blackjack players. When a stock drops in price, DeLamielleure actually buys more shares. This lowers his

❝ I look for erratic moves. If I see a stock just ticking along and all of a sudden there's a giant spike up and there's no news, I always short it. If there's a giant tick down, and there's no news, nine times out of ten I'll go long with the stock. ❞

per-share losses and lowers his average cost basis in the stock. Averaging down also allows him to profit faster when the stock reverses in price. As he explains, "If the stock's trading down on a tick chart I'll go in and buy 500 here. And if it drops another point, I'll go in for 1,000. And if it comes down a little more, I'll go in for another 500."

Of course, there's never a guarantee that the stock will reverse in price. Which makes averaging down a dangerous technique for all but skilled traders. The reason, of course, is that adding to a declining position – whatever it might do to your average cost basis – only exacerbates your total dollar loss. And the loss can be substantial if you're trading volatile $100-plus stocks. Reason enough why DeLamielleure prefers stocks in the $40 range.

"You can't trade like that [averaging down] if you trade $100 stocks," he says, "or you'll get your head ripped off. But you can trade more conservative stocks like $20 to $40 stocks. If a $30 stock is down 3 points and there's no news, there's a pretty good chance that it's not going to be down another 3 points in an hour or so. It's going to be down a point and a half." At which point DeLamielleure might elect to add to his core position. "Some of these stocks that are 150 bucks, potentially they could drop 50 points a day."

According to trading guru Robert Deel, author of The Strategic Electronic Day Trader, whose advice DeLamielleure follows, such trends are most likely to play out during the first two hours and the last two hours of each trading day, or from 9:30 to 11:30 A.M. and again from 2 to 4 P.M. Eastern Time (ET). As for the rest of the trading day – roughly from 11:30 A.M. to 2 P.M. ET – Deel refers to it as "the grinder, a time when the markets remain choppy and trends are difficult or impossible to discern."

Within this morning and afternoon trading window, Deel postulates that trends typically play out over 5, 15, 20, and 35 minutes. A 5-minute tick chart – the time frame used by DeLamielleure – is the best way of detecting these microtrends. If you zoom back – and use a 10-minute chart – you might miss a trend formation entirely. Similarly, if you zoom in close – say by using a 2-minute tick chart – the ultra-short-term trading patterns (what Deel calls "the aura of volatility") will likely send confusing signals. Moreover, institutional traders often use 2-minute charts, Deel says. Therefore, you time your own buy and sell signals in tandem with these heavy-sized traders, your own buy and sell orders will be over-whelmed like driftwood in a tidal wave. Ergo, Deel and his followers settle on a 5-minute chart as a way of forecasting a trend. To confirm that trend, they zoom out to a 15-minute chart. Once traders sense these subtle market movements, they use their turbo-charged software to descend on the stock like ravenous piranha. And that's the reason trends often exhaust themselves within minutes. Rarely will trends last over an hour, Deel says.

Deel tells traders not to anticipate or guess at a trend, but to wait until it actually occurs. For example, a stock might hang just below its resistance level while consolidating. Many traders might be tempted to buy it at this point, since this will enable them to ride the full breadth of its upward move. However, in the short term, stocks are just as likely to move down following a consolidation. Meaning, the trade could go against you.

One step forward, two steps back

These trend patterns, of course, play out both in choppy markets and in markets that are clearly trending. The difference is that in choppy markets the trends manifest themselves over the course of minutes. In strongly trending markets, they may play out over days – providing significantly higher payouts as a result.

Whatever the time frame, DeLamielleure uses a similar strategy to exploit the trend. If a stock is trending up and temporarily reverses, DeLamielleure will take advantage of the opportunity to add to his position. In a case where a stock is falling sharply – as occurred throughout the spring of 2000 – DeLamielleure will attempt to ride the stock back up during its tiny rallies and then sell after he's made what he considers an acceptable gain – which is usually 1 or 2 points, or about 3 to 5 percent of a $40 stock.

"A lot of times if I buy 1,000 shares of something, if it's running up, I'll offer it up at a point and a half higher and be happy with the profit. If it goes up 3 more points, then it sucks." In other words, if he sells, only to watch the stock continue to rise, it'll hurt for sure. Then again experienced traders know that the market continually serves up

> **" In a case where a stock is falling sharply ... DeLamielleure will attempt to ride the stock back up during its tiny rallies and then sell after he's made what he considers an acceptable gain – which is usually 1 or 2 points, or about 3 to 5 percent of a $40 stock. "**

fresh opportunities. "The bottom line with these things is that you can always get back in. They bounce and they come back. You won't get back in as cheap as before. But you'll still get the run-up."

Of course he's not always right. DeLamielleure says that when he guesses wrong "you just get a feeling like, man, this isn't good, and you'll see lots of selling on instinct and that's generally institutions" who are doing the selling, he says. "And then you can just tell." At that point he'll switch to a more defensive mode. "If a stock has gone down from $39 to $36 and your average cost is 36½ and you're kind of still sitting there, a lot of times it's just not moving and it's more than just an aberration. At times like that I will sell half my position and watch it carefully and then potentially sell it all. I don't have many down days, but those are my biggest down days."

Better safe than sorry

It's easy to see why DeLamielleure can rack up 50 trades per day, since he's constantly paring or adding to the core positions he maintains in 3-4 different stocks as he buys and sells 500- to 1,000-share blocks. He rarely holds positions larger than 3,000 shares. At any point in time he might have $300,000 or more committed to the market. It's a rare day for him to trade on margin. The rest of his trading cash normally sits in a money market account.

While he's trading, DeLamielleure stays in close touch – either by phone or e-mail – with people he calls his "trader buddies." "Everyone was in the business at one time or another," he says. "One guy was a trader at a hedge fund. One guy was a broker. We pretty much have a whole network. We give each other ideas. If you trade alone, you need ideas."

Many in this group trade far more aggressively than DeLamielleure.

"A lot of my trader buddies tell me that it's wrong," he says. The very fact that he has so few bad days proves he's not taking big enough risks in order to get the big rewards. "They trade huge size. They get 10-1. [That is, their margin requirement is only 10 percent versus 50 percent allowed most traders.] I could get 10-1 if I wanted to right now. I was talking to my buddy today at [a financial firm in Chicago] and they were getting the Greenspan talk over the tape a little bit early. And they went in and bought 20,000 QQQs ([index shares on the NASDAQ 100]. That's some serious jack. He made like $25,000 on it. Sometimes I wish I had more capital and bigger balls," DeLamielleure laments. "Because I could take down bigger size. For me to swing that much size I'd have to have a T1 connection. But I'm comfortable with what I'm doing. Today I didn't take anything long, because the market moved so much so quick. So I'll pretty much play it by ear on Monday."

Brendan Delamielleures's trading rules

- *Create a list of dominant stocks within a sector, being certain that the sector offers sufficient volatility for profitable trading.* Next, identify viable second-tier stocks within the sector. When a dominant stock begins to move, open a position in the second-tier stock, since it will likely move in the same direction. By focusing on second-tier stocks, you avoid the rush of other traders who jump in and out of sector leaders whenever they make significant moves. Second-tier stocks experience a slight delay in moving following a move by the major player. This affords traders the opportunity to get in early and capture a greater portion of the move.

- *Favor stocks trading in the $20-$40 range.* This allows you to build relatively large positions (500 – 3,000 shares) with less capital. Likewise you can avoid trading on margin. Stocks in the $20-$40 range rarely make extreme moves. Rarely do they lose $1/3$ to $1/2$ their value, for example. By contrast, stocks selling for $150 to $250 can move $30 or more per day, and falls of $50 to $75 aren't unusual.

- *Research the fundamentals of the second-tier stocks well in advanced of trading them.* That way you can move quickly and confidently to open a position. When researching fundamentals pay particular attention to the float – or the number of share available to trade – as well as the average volume. Stocks with greater floats tend to be less volatile and therefore less profitable to trade. Knowing average volume will alert you to unusual trading activity. Last, regularly study charts of the stocks both while trading and at the end of the day. Again, this will acquaint you with the stock's normal trading pattern and help alert you to anomalies.

- *Use a 5-minute bar chart to spot emerging trends.* To confirm the trend, zoom out to a 15-minute chart, paying close attention to support and resistance levels.

- *Look for stocks that are attempting to find a bottom.* But be aware that finding a precise bottom is often difficult. For that reason you should build your positions gradually by averaging down. If a $30 stock has fallen $3 on the opening to $27, you might, for example, open a position with 500 shares. If it falls another point or two, buy an additional 500 to 1,000 shares. If it falls lower than you expected, sell half the position and continue to watch the stock closely. However, if it bounces hold on until it moves up 1 or 1½ points above your original entry point. Again, 5-minute tick charts will identify these short-term trends, which can be confirmed using a 15-minute chart.

Chapter Four
Those Who Forget the Past . . .
Terry Bruce: Gap Trader*

During particularly bad times – like, say, when his end-of-month trading account balance shows a $20,000 loss – Terry Bruce takes solace in the fact that even the very best traders have sometimes blown out their capital on their road to riches. And sometimes they've done it more than once. Bruce, 51, who makes his home in Seattle, has seen his share of spectacular ups and downs, too. Back in 1996, in just six months' time, he grew a $75,000 account into $575,000. Incredibly, a little over one year later the account crashed to zero. And Bruce found himself living on a $14,000 personal line of credit. To get back into the game, he gave up his job, took out a second mortgage on his house, and resolved never to make the same mistakes again.

The silence of the web

To follow Bruce's roller-coaster investment career, let's go back to the mid-'90s. The bull market's been steaming along. But Bruce was totally out of the game. Instead in that era, which marked the rise of the day trader, he was earning a decent living as a photographer, shooting products, fashion models, or food – whatever it took to pay the bills. Now, it's worth reflecting that there are certain uncanny similarities between photography and day trading. Both are male-dominated professions. Both professions also tend to attract free-spirited, creative types. Also, both professions require a similar amount of start-up capital. A professional photographer might easily spend $40,000 to $50,000 on lenses, lights, and other rudimentary studio equipment. That's also about the

---

*At the subject's request, this name is a pseudonym.

minimum stake needed for day trading. Moreover, the return on capital for photographers and day traders tends to be very similar, too. A good photographer bills at about $1,500 per day. (Though most experience profitless days – or worse, days when they lose money.) The key point is that during the course of a year, a good photographer can get a 200-400 percent return off a $50,000 investment. A skilled day trader might do about the same.

Problem was, Bruce had been doing photography for close to 20 years. And he felt himself getting burned out. "I didn't want to be a photographer for the rest of my life," he says. "It's more a job for young people. It's high energy. There's a lot of hauling equipment around. It's a lot of work." Plus it's a feast or famine business, he says. "You make good money when you're busy. But the when it slows down you go crazy for a month or so and wonder if you'll ever get anymore work."

Some traders might say the same thing about their ability to make profits in choppy markets. But regardless, one of the second careers Bruce looked into was stockbroker. However, he soon realized that he could probably make more trading his own account than he could charging his clients commission. At least it was worth a try. Taking $75,000, essentially his retirement savings, Bruce set up an account with JB Oxford (www.jboxford.com) and began trading from a laptop in his studio.

Like a lot of traders in those early days, and now, Bruce started with very little preparation. Twenty years ago, he might have subscribed to a newsletter and followed its editor's picks to the letter. But with the advent of the Internet, a new breed of stock guru was emerging. And many were giving advice for free online. "Where I learned the most was on AOL from Rev. Shark," Bruce says. Rev. Shark (a.k.a. Jim De Porre) was one of the original online gurus to establish a chat site where active traders could compare strategies and ideas.

A former Michigan attorney, De Porre was forced to give up a promising practice at age 30, when doctors told him he was going deaf. Not the kind of person to give up easily, De Porre found the silence of the Web to be his natural medium – just as online investing became a natural profession. And he has reportedly earned millions at it. Offering his often caustic yet insightful views first on Motley Fool and then on AOL at his forum Shark Attack, De Porre became something of a legend among day traders. He has since teamed up with another trader profiled in this book. Scott Slutsky (see page 109). The two have their own paid chat site, SuperTraders.com.

In any event, Shark Attack on AOL was where Bruce chose to hang out. When a fellow poster mentioned a stock Bruce would look up its chart. And in that way he learned some of the basic concepts employed by active traders, things like support and resistance levels and moving averages. Bruce also dabbled in stochastics, convergence/divergences, and MACD histrograms. Each of these indicators – little known by those unfamiliar with technical analysis – plot the average price for a stock over a set period of time. Then through intricate mathematical means, they attempt to show at what points during the test period the stock might be overbought or oversold. Done by hand the necessary calculations would take hours. But PC-based technical analysis programs can render illuminating charts in seconds. And in fact, by the mid-'90s these tools were becoming readily available on the Web.

Bruce says that his initial exposure to technical indicators helped him "become much more knowledgeable about where to get in and out of positions." But in the end, he opted to simplify his trading strategy as much as he could. "It gets too complicated when you get too many indicators going," he says. Instead, Bruce chose to focus on basics, such as moving averages and volume. "I looked at support areas and I looked at volume and I attempted to trade with the trend of the market," he says.

The market would prove extraordinarily kind – at least at first. "It was mostly buy and hold," he recalls. Like several other traders profiled in this book, Bruce sought to build core positions in stocks he liked. Then he would add or delete blocks of stocks, in effect averaging up or down to reduce his per-share loss or maximize per-share profitability.

One stock that treated Bruce especially well was Iomega (IOM). "I had about 10,000 shares of Iomega," he remembers. "That thing split about four to five times while I held it. I started with 1,200 shares. I'd buy 300 or 400 shares, then I'd buy maybe another couple of hundred, when I'd get more confident about it. So I had most of my money in that one stock. Then as I started making money in that stock, I started buying others." Namely other technology and Internet plays popular at the time, such as AOL and Lycos (LYCOS).

By spring of '96, Bruce's account had grown to $575,000. Not bad considering he was working full-time as a photographer the whole while. "It was the technology craze," he says, thinking back. "I thought – geez – these stocks were going pretty good. They're going to be long-term holds. You could hang on to them, and even though there would be dips they would come back."

Bruce found his confidence growing more or less in tandem with his account balance. And then, like a lot of traders, he discovered that too much confidence is definitely not a good thing. Daily gains of $1,000 or $2,000 – the bread and butter profits of successful day traders no longer seemed worth the trouble.

Bruce found himself taking bigger and bigger risks, buying bigger blocks of share with each trade. And when he guessed wrong, instead of exiting the position immediately, as most trading coaches would advise, Bruce hung on, refusing to take the loss – even as the size of that loss grew with each downtick.

In the end, just as Iomega had carried his account to new heights, its downfall brought him crashing back to Earth. "There was a top in May '96," Bruce remembers. "Then stocks corrected. Iomega was in the 50s at that point. It dropped about 10 points. So when you've got 10,000 shares that's quite a hit," he says. One hundred grand to be exact.

Iomega's fall is perhaps a casebook study of how yesterday's no-end-in-sight technology stock can become today's market pariah. The company specialized in high-density memory storage devices. And to an army of pundits it seemed as if the company had a lock on a market that might never stop growing. After all, computer files of all kinds were growing fatter by the month. As simple documents incorporated spreadsheets and graphics, even sound and videos, simple floppy disks no longer sufficed. A single floppy disk, for example, could no longer hold a high-resolution photograph. So Iomega's drives and high-density floppies rightfully belonged on everyone's desktop. Or so the thinking went. Growth in Iomega's share price largely helped propel the model portfolio run by the Motley Fool's Gardner Brothers to over a 1,000 percent return. And many an early tech trader likewise grew rich on the stock.

But just as in an earlier age, when a completely new technology (the telegraph) blew out a much-heralded old one (the Pony Express), Iomega was rendered a virtual non-contender by the Internet. Everyone with a PC could now port themselves into a single humongous network. And that meant files of several megabytes could be easily passed from user to user simply by clicking the send button on a Web browser. For Iomega the final blow probably came with the advent of writable CD-ROMs; costing less than $2 each, they could hold 640 megabytes of data.

Savvy investors realized years in advance that shortly every computer sold would have a CD-ROM burning capability built in. A vicious selling frenzy ensued. Bruce remembers that after it first drop Iomega fluctuated around for a while. And then one day it made another big drop into the low 30s, then the high 20s. "It took about two months for the market to bottom out," he says. At the time this book went to press, the stock was trading at just over $6 per share.

For Bruce, the easy money days appeared over. But even bigger losses loomed ahead. "When I lost all that money, I thought, 'Geez, I've got to make it back.'

So I started taking bigger positions in shares of $50 stocks. And if it dropped down, I wouldn't sell it quick enough and I'd lose a few thousand."

In addition to Iomega, all the other stocks Bruce owned seemed locked in a kamikaze dive. His entire portfolio was evaporating before his eyes. "I don't remember exactly how things played out," he says ruefully. "After screwing around trading over a period of a year, I took all that money and just blew it. Just kind of frittered it away. My account was about down to zero. I think I had about $14,000 in one account. And that was money I borrowed on a line of credit."

Don't try this at home

So there went the retirement nest egg and maybe a lot of Bruce's confidence. Bruce, of course, still had his photography business. "There was one quote I liked," he says, attempting to remember the exact wording. "I asked God for riches, but I might be happy if he gave me poverty so that I may be wise." So I just read that and said that maybe this is for a reason. That was in '98 and I thought this would be good time to do some more learning."

Bruce pored through investment books and financial magazines, as well as investment newsletters. He stayed up nights examining stock charts. The loss made him more determined than ever to come back. "For some reason I just felt I could do this," he says. "I felt somewhere in me that it could be done."

Bruce was so determined to succeed, he broke the most fundamental rule of trading. He put his own house on the line. The equity in his home amounted to somewhere north of $40,000. Bruce borrowed on all of it. He used some of the money to pay down his personal loan. The rest went into his trading account.

With his second chance to score in the market, and with everything riding on it, Bruce vowed not to make the mistakes that had punished him before. This time around, Bruce devised some clear-cut rules for himself. "I just saw trading in a different light," he says. He would focus solely on the indicators he trusted most: support and resistance levels along with volume. At the same time he would curb his greed. No more huge positions, no more ridiculous risks. Think small, he told himself. "I said, 'If I can make $200 per day that comes out to $50,000 per year.' And I thought $200 per day really isn't very much. I should be able to do that by doing small trades. That really helped." In fact, most day trading coaches advise their students to do just that when they've suffered a loss. Take down smaller positions; focus on sustainable goals. Protect your profits. And most of all, rebuild your confidence.

Running the gap

Bruce also realized that if he was going to succeed as a trader he needed to approach it as a full-time job. Too many times in the past he had gone out on a photography assignment and earned $1,500 for the day, and would return that evening to his studio to find that his losses in the market far exceeded any profits he'd made in photography. If he'd been there, paying attention he might have sold at a critical time or bought that stock that was making a steep climb just before the close. If only he'd been there.

To give himself that needed time, Bruce scaled back his photography business. But of course that also meant that trading would become his sole source of income. Not only that, but his trading capital less than $40,000 – would have to pay back two mortgages and cover his other living expenses. Little wonder, he admits, "I was gun shy. I was really nervous about stocks dropping, so I tended to sell things quick," he says. "In a way that was a good thing because it made me more careful."

With any other business it would have been impossible to build profits so quickly. But a skilled trader – at least in theory – can begin earning money from day one. And that's what happened with Bruce. He honed in, making small trades. At first he refused to commit all his capital to the market. "I might commit it for a day or two," he says. "I would buy enough stocks if I was confident in the market to ensure that a few of them would move," he says. Also, he was loath to trade on margin at first, for fear of exacerbating his losses.

"Occasionally at first I wouldn't be able to sleep well that first fall when I was trading," he says. "I'd be worried about my positions."

Fortunately once again the market proved kind. By fall it had begun to rise. Bruce's confidence rose, too – enough that he began using margin. The victories multiplied. At one point he owned 800 shares of the cable ISP @home (ATHM, now Excite@Home), which netted him 20 points or $16,000.

But mostly it was the smaller trades that Bruce ground out that grew his account dollar by dollar. To spread his risk around, he'd hold maybe 20 stocks at a time. Using that short gun approach, he'd quickly sell any losers and hold on to the winners for as long as they continued to rise. As a result, Bruce found himself making 20-50 trades in the course of a day and paying out as much as $450 per day in commissions. Which of course meant that to realize even his modest goal of $200 in profits per day he'd need to generate $650.

As before, most of Bruce's trades amounted to pruning his positions, adding shares, selling shares, protecting his profits, nipping a loss in the bud. Most of the stocks in his portfolio were in the $20-$40 range. And he'd seldom own more than 1,000 shares of any one stock. "It seemed like every time I'd take a larger position, I'd get scared and sell if there was a downtick. So I'd sell and miss the gains.

Bruce didn't have any hard and fast rules about when he'd exit a losing position, although usually he only let it drop a point or two.

One of Bruce's highest percentage trades was the so-called gap play. This is a long position entered near the end of the day and held overnight, in the hope that the stock would rise further from its closing prices during the next day's trading – that it would "gap up", in other words, In choppy markets the gap trade has become increasingly important to traders. This is because often the market will make its biggest move in the morning. Following the opening move, stocks will either settle back or hold whatever gains they made at the open.

Precisely because they require traders to hold long positions overnight, gap trades tend to be risky. Unexpected news released after the close can rock the market the next morning. But even in the absence of news, the market open is the most treacherous time to trade. In the hours and minutes before the opening bell, only the NASDAQ market makers know how many buy and sell orders they have for a particular stock. While on the New York Stock Exchange (NYSE), only the specialists know at what price the stock will open. (For an explanation of how market makers and specialists do their jobs, see chapter 7 on Chris Farrell.) Individual traders, by contrast, remain in the dark until the opening bell, their Level II screens in those pre-opening moments all but useless. Consequently, most readers simply sit back and wait for the opening chaos to sort itself out. And this can take anywhere from 10 minutes to an hour or more on especially frenetic days.

Despite these handicaps, Bruce became skilled enough at gap trading to make it one of the more potent weapons in his arsenal. Searching for stocks that are likely gap candidates on any given day, he looks for certain key signs, "If a stock looks like it's got good volume near the close, if it's on an up trend, that would make me tend to want to hold it," he says. He also pays attention to the broader market: "Total market volume should be healthy. Stocks in the sector should look good."

But not too good: "If the market is on a big trend day" – meaning maybe a rise of 100 points or more – "I like to see how the stock closes," he says. "A lot of times when it closes it sells off at the end." If that's the case, Bruce says, "there's a better chance for a gap to occur the next day because most of the sellers are out. But if it closes on a huge run, then sometimes it's exhausted. And the next it doesn't gap up." Personally, Bruce says, "I like to see a neutral close rather than huge price run at the end of the day." However, if it looked like a lot of traders were exiting their positions, he might become a buyer in the hope of being rewarded with a gap up the following morning.

Gap ups can be especially profitable. A 3-point gap, which is not unusual for momentum stocks, could consequently result in a $3,000 gain on a 1,000-share position – nice way to start the trading day, even if that day did start at 6:30 A.M. in Seattle. Problem is, it's tough to pinpoint exactly which stocks will make their move. So like a sports handicapper, Bruce spread his bets around.

If you have 10 stocks, you're bound to have a few of them gapping," he says. "Some of them might open flat but you're not going to lose anything on them. You can usually get out.

And what about the stocks that do gap up? "Then you have to decide whether you're going to sell the gap," explains Bruce. "If I think it has a chance to run, I'll sell half my position and keep half." Again, this is a risky play, because stocks tend to be at their most volatile in the morning. Bruce might put in a limit order to sell half his position before the open. Or else he'll enter a market order at the open price. The latter can sting even the most skilful traders, once again because of the extreme volatility at the open. But Bruce insists he's successful more often than not. "If there a lot of sellers you might get a little worse than the open price," he says. But "sometimes you get really good prices, right on the high tick."

Dollar by dollar, Bruce's gap trades and his day trades again pushed his account back toward respectability. Soon he found that he was doing a lot better than $200 per day. In fact, by the start of 1999 his account totalled $220,000, thanks in part to a generally upbeat market. And from there, it kept rolling. In January 1999, one of his better months, he made $100,000. And by that time he even felt confident enough to take some time off – or at least try to.

I was in Miami for one week with some buddies," Bruce recounts. "I took my laptop. And I traded using that. I think I made about $55,000 in that week.

Back to seven figures

Bruce says he went out at night with the guys. But otherwise he stayed holed up in his hotel room. "I had my own room. So I was pretty much on my own." The guys slept in from their nights out. Bruce shied away from any heavy drinking for fear a hangover would impair his trading. First thing each morning he opened up his laptop and ported up. "I never saw the beach once in my whole trip to Miami," he says. Holed up inside all day he began to think "I could have been anywhere. I'm here in Miami, and all I'm doing is staring at my computer."

Sometimes you have to lose money before you can really learn how to trade. Because learning how to trade teaches you how not to lose money. By learning how not to lose money, I was able to make money.

Along came February, and the market turned choppy. Bruce remembers how he "really felt kind of frustrated." He lost $20,000 that month. "What am I doing wrong?" The question nagged at him. Bruce found that at such times, "It helps to read other people's comments, like [James} Cramer on TheStreet.com. I found that a lot of people were having the same problems. They were doing the same things they were doing in January, and it wasn't working for them."

Still as thousand-dollar losses ticked off his portfolio by the hour, Bruce couldn't help wondering if his jinx was returning. "I thought, 'What if I go the rest of the year and I can't make any more money?' You think maybe the markets never going to get good again. Maybe I'll never be able to make money again. You kind of think that way. I felt like I was cautious enough that I wasn't about to make the same mistakes as before. Plus I'd read that a lot of successful traders have gone bankrupt in their careers."

Thankfully, things turned around during March and April. In June, Bruce remembers making $30,000. Then summer arrived and the markets turned choppy again. But looming in the wings was autumn – the early dawn of the new millennium. Bruce rode the market's dizzying up trend through the end of '99. He'd made approximately $480,000 during the year. And that was not counting the money he'd taken from his account to pay the bills, not the money he needed to pay down his loans. Although his account totalled roughly $700,000 by the start of the new millennium, Bruce still hadn't paid off his home equity loan.

But no matter, the market continued its extraordinary rise into the first weeks of 2000. And it was around then that Bruce's portfolio topped seven figures. Although the moment didn't come as any kind of magical revelation. "I was trading three accounts at the time," Bruce says. For that reason, he says he can't be certain exactly when the three together reached the magic number. At its height, Bruce's account topped $1.2 million. And by that time he realized he'd reached an important milestone. "It really didn't change my life that much," he says. "But it made me feel like this was a great way to make a living and I could be really successful at it. I could be more successful than most people, and a lot of my hard work had paid off." To celebrate, he bought a new BMW 540.

> **" Initially I wanted to make $200 per day. Then I got the point where I was making $1,000 a day and maybe $2,000. During the beginning of the year, when the market was going really crazy, I was averaging $10,000 or $12,000 a day. "**

We all know what happened next, of course. The market that had exceeded all expectations reversed course and plunged to depths no one would have dreamed possible. Like so many other traders, Bruce saw his account hemorrhage money from every pore. But thinking back on it, Bruce blames only himself for the huge losses he suffered. Once again, he had allowed himself to get too cocky. And as a result, he repeated many of the same mistakes that had caused his downfall just two years earlier. Bruce's own explanation of what happened would no doubt be echoed by many traders who blew out their accounts in the cruel spring of 2000.

"I got a little too confident," he says. "When I saw my account dropping I tried to make up for it a little too quickly by taking bigger positions. I got away from what had helped me out in the beginning. I got away from the philosophy of just making a small amount each day and being satisfied with it. Initially I wanted to make $200 per day. Then I got the point where I was making $1,000 a day and maybe $2,000. During the beginning of the year, when the market was going really crazy, I was averaging $10,000 or $12,000 a day."

Conversely, with an account balance rife with zeros, large losses didn't sting quite as badly as they should have. "Even when the market was going down," Bruce says, "1,000 bucks a day didn't seem like that much any more. I tried to make the money back in the wrong kind of market, instead of pulling back and waiting till the thing settled out."

Perhaps because Bruce had grown wise from his losses in the past, that was exactly how he managed to staunch his haemorrhaging account before the losses proved crippling. At its lowest point, Bruce figured he dropped $400,000. Which still left him with $800,000 to trade with – a phenomenal return even factoring in the loss, when you consider that it was milked from a mere $40,000 and that Bruce had to pay $450 per day in commissions and keep himself in spending money. More important, despite the choppy market conditions that continued well into 2000, he managed to steadily rebuild his positions, using gap trades and swing trades as his chief weapons.

A good chunk of his money also sits in his long-term trading account. And one of his revelations from the spring downfall was that technology stocks – owing to their volatility – tend to make poor long-term holds. So he is attempting to diversify out of the tech stocks that hit him the hardest during the 2000 crash. In addition to that long-term portfolio, Bruce maintains two separate accounts, one for swing trading and one for day trading. And he says his day trading account has performed the best of the three. Like other traders profiled in this book, he's been forced to seek out tiny intraday trends and wait while the market searches for a trend that's long-term and firm. It's the kind of market where he must reluctantly take bigger risks than he has in the past if he's to realize any profits at all. And the goal of $200 per day profit seems permanently in the past. "I still try to make bigger amounts than I used to." So too, maybe, is Bruce's propensity to take inordinate risks of the kind that cost him so heavily in the past. "A lot of times I'll be invested overnight," he says. "And the next day I'll sell off everything and just sit back and see what's going on."

Terry Bruce's trading rules

- *Make trading your full-time job if you expect to earn significant gains.* You must watch the market every day to be in synch with it.

- *Limit the number of indicators you watch when trading.* Pay close attention to support and resistance and volume. And always know the trend of the market you're trading in.

- *If you suffer a setback, go back to square one.* Set modest goals for yourself, such as the amount of money you wish to make each day.

- *Hold positions overnight when you expect a gap up the following day.* Oftentimes the best indication of a gap up is if the stock trades higher all day and on a day when the market rises by 150 points. Then look for a sell-off at the day's end. If the sell-off does occur this should rid the stock of sellers, giving buyers dominance when the market reopens the following day. Conversely, a stock that rallies at the end of the day might succumb to selling pressure the following day.

- *If the stock appears to be heading higher after a gap up at the open, consider selling half the position to preserve your gain.*

- *Technology stocks are mainly for trading; because of their volatility they make poor long-term holds.*

- *Pay attention to general indicators,* like money flowing into the market, to give you a general feeling for any medium-term trend. Use this information to help you decide whether or not to take positions overnight.

- *Hold positions in 20 or so stocks on the premise that some will rise, others will remain flat, and still others will fall.* Quickly exit losing positions. Hold on to flat stocks for a reasonable time. And continue to hold winners until they appear to have peaked.

- *Exit positions when they drop by 1 or 1½ points.*

- *Rarely hold more than 1,000 share of a stock.*

- *Rarely trade your entire account,* unless you're certain the market is strongly trending upward.

Chapter Five
Trading As a Quest for Knowledge
Oliver Velez: The Teacher

Oliver Velez is one of the traders who makes it all look deceptively easy. In addition to trading part-time, he also runs several companies, all of which can be accessed from the Web site Pristine.com, a popular portal for active traders. The main focus of those companies is on teaching the craft of trading as well as supplying the tools traders use. Make that traders around the globe. Pristine's editors translate much of the site's content into Spanish, Japanese, and German.

If all that weren't enough to keep him busy, Velez travels frequently in connection with his job. One week he might be speaking at a traders' convention such as the Online Trading Expo. Another week you'll find him in Miami, helping promote one of his business ventures, a site devoted to Hispanic traders.

So how well does he do at trading part-time? Astonishingly well, it turns out. In the course of his trading career, Velez claims to have taken millions from the market. Although he is uncomfortable discussing specific amounts, some of his trades are deliberately documented so that his students can learn from them.

"One of the things I try to do each year is take a $50,000 account and show individuals what can be done with that small amount of money. In 1999, I took that $50,000 to over $500,000, trading on average a couple of hours a day." True enough, 1999 was a spectacular year for the markets. The top-earning mutual fund during the period, the Nicholas-Applegate Global Technology Class I, returned 494 percent. But that was less than half the 10-fold increase Velez experienced. And Velez achieved his results despite the fact he quit trading for four months in order to write a book. What's more, he often resorted to trading from hotel rooms, using a laptop. He keeps a list of hotels around the world that offer guests easy access to the Internet. For those of us who believe our lives are too frenetic to trade actively, Velez is clearly a guy worth paying attention to.

As for his trading style, Velez seems to especially like swing trading. A swing trader holds on to a select group of relatively large positions in hope that they'll move up 5 to 10 percent or so in the course of one or two weeks. Velez will tell you that swing traders occupy a unique niche among traders as a whole. Day traders focus on fractional moves that occur in the course of a single trading day. And they're loath to hold a position overnight. Instead, they sell all their holdings and revert to cash by the end of each trading day. On the opposite end of the spectrum, you find the majority of institutional traders – those who manage mutual funds, pension funds, and the like. Institutional investors look for stocks to move over the course of months, even years. Which puts swing traders nicely in the middle, Velez believes. And because of their unique niche, they seldom find themselves trading against either group.

In practice, Velez likes to hold no more than five positions at a time. More typically he limits his positions to two. "I know of some traders who hold 400 positions at the same time," he says. "They in effect become the market. My style calls for me to take a very concentrated approach." Naturally, whatever positions he takes tend to be huge. And he'll unremorsefully dump a position if it doesn't perform as expected. Often he'll do this after just five consecutive trading days. Never mind if the stock's moving up. If it's not moving up fast enough, Velez will look elsewhere for a stock that'll work his capital harder. The market, as the saying goes, constantly serves up fresh opportunities.

Birth of an anti-fundamentalist

Before you can understand the specific methods Velez uses, however, you need to understand the man. Velez says his own education as a trader goes back to the mid-'80s, the height of the leveraged buyout boom. Fortunes were made by speculators who correctly guessed which company might be acquired next. "It was a very exciting time" to be in the markets, he recalls. Velez who'd been fascinated with the markets, during his college years, recalls reading a magazine article one day on investment clubs. In an investment club, members pool their money each month. And they decide by voting what stocks to buy or sell. Velez was working as an accountant at the time. Barely out of college and still in what was basically an entry-level job, he didn't have much money to invest. But an investment club, which could pool his and others' funds, offered a way around that. So Velez decided to start one of his own.

"Like most people," he says, "I primarily focused on a long-term approach." He thought his accounting background would give him an edge at analyzing the fundamentals of companies. But it didn't work out that way.

"Over a period of time, I did exceptionally poorly. I found that the fundamental approach really had a great many holes." While he continued to invest, and grew more adept at his day job as bean counter, it dawned on Velez precisely why fundamental analysis was flawed. What was an accountant after all, if not someone paid to "make the numbers look better than they actually were"? Velez realized. As he explains it, accountants manage this in a variety of ways: by "moving things into certain quarters, by delaying a certain posting, by taking advantage of certain loopholes." As a result, "a very falsified picture of the company could be presented for some time."

Rigging the books – and we're still talking here about methods that are perfectly legal – has if anything gotten worse since the mid-'80s. Freshly minted tech companies, especially those trafficking on the Internet, are among the most culpable. UCLA Finance Professor Ivo Welch and colleagues studied hundreds of newly IPOed companies and discovered that many used a rarefied form of accounting to add bounce to their balance sheets. The method, known as "positive accrual," allowed companies to account for expenses as bills are paid while stating earnings based on receivables – instead of when payments were actually received. Using positive accrual, earnings may appear to exceed cash flow. "There's quite a lot of 'earnings management' going on," Welch says ruefully. He advises investors to focus on cash flow, which is hard for companies to disguise.

So why haven't investors raised a stink? "It's almost expected," Welch says. "The NASD and the SEC are fully aware that these are new companies that want to look good when they step into the market, and they're not going to put forward their most conservative forecasting."

Some companies continue using this rarefied accounting practice for three months or more following an IPO, he says - enough time for VCs, investment banks, and management to legally sell their own shares. It's at this point, he says, that share prices plummet as the public gleans the real numbers for the first time.

Future perfect

Velez intuitively came to the same conclusion more than a decade ago. "Ultimately, "he says, "these things will be found out by the markets." However, often the discovery comes "too late for a lot of investors."

As time went on, Velez came to realize that fundamental analysis had an even deeper intrinsic flaw. "It's a snapshot of the company months ago. It is never an accurate picture of the company at the present moment and it doesn't come close to depicting the company in the future," he says. By contrast, the market is a discounting mechanism. Stocks of companies trade on the idea of where a company will be several months in the future.

Indeed, the same is true of markets as a whole. A significant point, since some people estimate that overall market trends can be responsible for as much as 80 percent of the moves made by individual stocks. As trading becomes more and more volatile, and as more investors clamber to get in, the market inevitably becomes even more forward-looking as all these traders seek first mover-advantage. Throughout much of the summer of '99, for example, markets waited tensely for a sign of just how badly the Y2K bug would affect companies' future earnings. Many analysts at the time predicted that a rally would take place several months into the year 2000, after the full effects of Y2K were known. However by the fall of 1999, it became generally known that Y2K's effects would be minimal. At that point the rally commenced in earnest. By the start of year 2000 that rally was in its last stages, and the markets began churning as big holders saw a top and exited before the April crash. Similarly, in the months following the crash, analysts predicted the market would continue to search for a bottom, until the Federal Reserve signalled that it was done raising interest rates. By early summer 2000, no such signal was heard. But markets commenced a short-term rally nonetheless, as traders became convinced that economic data would prompt the Fed to quit raising rates.

Years before any of this, Velez became firmly convinced that the indicators, the news, all the noise surrounding the markets were mainly distractions. What mattered was the simple movement of price as depicted on the charts. "So I began to delve into a more technical approach," he says. "And my performance started to improve."

The man on the bus and the doctor

Technical analysts believe that all the information available about a company has already been collectively priced into a stock, thanks to the constant process of buying and selling traders engage in. At their most extreme, technical analysts believe research into a company's earnings, its management or whatever is futile. All that matters are the patterns formed by the daily interaction of buyers and sellers. Often those patterns are analyzed using the same tools used by academics to study weather data or the likelihood that certain chemical reactions will take place. While many would call technical analysis a voodoo science, you'd be hard pressed to find a major brokerage house or institutional trading firm that didn't have its corps of technical analysts.

Thinking back on it, Velez says he learned about technical analysis almost by accident. He was riding a bus on the way to work one morning sitting next to a stranger. Somehow the two began talking about the markets. And Velez must have let on that he used fundamental analysis. At which point the man told Velez, "I've made a lot of money in the market. But I've never really approached the market as a fundamentalist." Instead, as Velez recalls, "The fellow started drawing these lines on a sheet of paper to show me." Velez became fascinated. "As a result of my conversation with this gentleman I went out and bought Dr Alexander Elder's *Trading for a Living*. It revolutionized my entire view of the market."

The founder of Elder.com, a trader's advisory firm based in Jackson Heights, New York, Elder is an enigmatic and revered figure among traders. He was born in St. Petersburg, Russia. At the age of 16 he was accepted into medical school. After graduation, Elder served as a doctor aboard a Soviet ship. When the ship was docked in Africa, Elder saw his opportunity and escaped. Eventually, he received political asylum in the United States. There his career branched off into several directions. While working in private practice as a psychiatrist, Elder also taught at Columbia University and for a time was employed as book editor of the *Psychiatric Times*. At the same time he found himself increasingly attracted to trading. Indeed, he quickly saw how a psychiatric background could become a unique asset to a trader. And he developed a strategy for traders that drew upon both their own psyche and the psychological forces underlying market movements. "The market is a loosely organized crowd," he writes in *Trading for a Living*." People change when they join crowds. They become more credulous and impulsive, they anxiously search for a leader, and react to emotions instead of using their intellect."

Elder reasoned that success at trading results from three crucial factors – mind, methods, and money. Just like a sports psychologist, he stresses in his seminars and consultations that traders first must develop winning attitudes in order to achieve success. Next they learn to use technical analysis to develop a strategy that suits them. The third key to success is the ability to manage trading capital.

Velez bought into the message. In particular, he became engrossed in Elder's analysis of chart reading. "Most traders use charts as a giant Rorschach test," Elder writes. He was referring, of course, to the inkblot tests long used by psychologists. "They project their hopes, fears, and fantasies onto the charts." To overcome these biases, Elder provided a more objective way to look at charts – a way based on psychological forces at work. "Support and resistance exist because people have memories," he writes. "Our memories prompt us to buy and sell at certain levels." His methods also introduced Velez to ideas like trading ranges and breakouts. "A chart reveals that markets spend most of their time in trading ranges. They spend less time in trends."

Mutual funds and the phases of the moon

Utilizing Elder's book as a departure point, Velez went on a kind of mental journey that took him deeper and deeper into the field of technical analysis. "In my quest for a level of mastery in markets I have studied virtually every possible approach in existence," he says. "There's a level of technical analysis that gets to the point of being ridiculous," Velez admits. Indeed, occasionally, there is an almost mystical quality to it as well. Fibonacci numbers, for example, originated with a thirteenth-century mathematician of the same name. 'To compute a series of Fibonacci numbers, start with the number 2 and add it to the previous number. For example, $2 + 1 = 3$ and $3 + 2 = 5$. From there on, whenever you add two consecutive numbers in the series together you arrive at the next number in the series. So $3 + 5 = 8$ and $8 + 5 = 13$. And so on. You can build a chain for as long as you like. But oddly enough, these numbers will all share certain relationships. As Martin J. Pring notes in his book *Technical Analysis Explained*, the ratio of the lower number in a series to the next higher is 61.8 to 100, while the ratio of the higher to the lower number is 161.8 to 100. All this would be complete psychobabble were it not for the fact that over the years people have discovered that these numbers mysteriously duplicate patterns found in nature. For example, the number of curves within a sunflower total 89, with 55 curving in one direction and 34 curving in the opposite direction. This corresponds exactly to three consecutive Fibonacci numbers: 34, 55, and 89. Likewise 13 keys make up an octave on a piano, denoting how Western musicians differentiate tones: five of those keys are black, eight are white. Again this corresponds to the consecutive Fibonacci numbers 5, 8 and 13. Odder still, tree branches multiply from the main tree trunk in Fibonacci series. An entire school of technical analysis called "Elliot Wave Theory" looks for additional manifestations of these patterns, particularly how they correspond to the rise and fall of markets.

Velez, too, became entranced with the patterns he found in charts. "Once I started to study charts, I became fanatical about it. I studied into the wee hours of the morning," he says. "Analyzing charts is like a doctor looking at x rays. After a while you begin to see the same patterns repeating over and over."

> **❝ To Velez, price and volume are somewhat antiseptic terms for describing what really occurs when stocks trade. In Velez's vision, every day in the markets a dramatic battle takes place between buyers and sellers. ❞**

One of the patterns Velez discovered was that the middle of the month often proved to be a turning point for many stocks. For example, if a stock moved up during the first couple of weeks of a month, it might head down for the remainder of the month. "There are some really weird theories regarding this," Velez says. "Astrologers believe it's because in the middle of the month you tend to have a lot of full moons." But, he says, a lot of seasoned traders believe the phenomenon results from the way mutual funds deal with their money. Many times mutual funds receive their cash inflows at the beginning of the month. Similarly, a lot of 401 (k) plans collect the money all month and send it as a lump sum to mutual funds – again often at the beginning of the month. Mutual funds are required by their prospectuses to put that money to work. So the first couple of weeks tend to produce excessive buying. "Of course," Velez says, "when it's over, that level of buying dries up a little bit until the next cash infusion."

The battle rages

From his broad-ranging search, Velez was successful at honing down the field of technical analysis to some core concepts that would serve him well.

"Whenever you move very far away from what really counts," he says, "you're moving into dangerous waters." What really counts, in this case, is price and volume. Moreover, to Velez, price and volume are somewhat antiseptic terms for describing what really occurs when stocks trade. In Velez's vision, every day in the markets a dramatic battle takes place between buyers and sellers. A trader need only focus on two points he says: "when the buyers take control back from the sellers, and when the sellers take control back from the buyers."

An equally important concept is that those buyers and sellers are not abstractions on a chart, but real people. "One of the key things that I teach all over the world is that we do not trade stocks; we trade people. What a lot of knowledgeable market players fail to realize is that there is someone on the other side of every single transaction you make. The question always becomes, Who's smarter? Is it you or the person on the other side?"

To be successful at trading you must be the smarter one on the majority of occasions, Velez says. It's that simple.

Trading is nothing more than finding two groups of ill-informed market players, those willing to give up their merchandise at a price you know is too inexpensive, and those willing to buy your merchandise at a price you know is too expensive.

While Velez was developing these ideas, he was given a unique opportunity to test them. The firm where he worked as an accountant let him manage part of a $40-million hedge fund. This occurred during the late '80s. Markets were still reeling from the crash of '87. And there was a decent amount of volatility. Velez remembers. But nothing, of course fore-shadowed the long-running bull market that would commence in the early '90s. Still, over a 2½ period during the late '80s, Velez achieved 38 percent annual gains. At the time he himself was making roughly $38,000 a year, he recalls, while he estimates he was making his firm's clients $30,000 per hour. Velez asked his employers for a raise. When they refused, he quit.

Small chips in a big game

Newly married, and out on his own, Velez nevertheless
take some big risk if he was to succeed. He found two backei.
give him $20,000 each in trading capital. His wife cashed in her ⌐
gave him another $4,000. Velez then took his $44,000 stake to a propⅰ.
trading firm – he'd rather not name it – that based on his record gave him 1ʋ
to 1 leverage on his capital. In effect, this meant that the money in his account
was put in escrow. And he basically traded the firm's money. The leverage
amounted to nearly half a million. The terms of his relationship with the firm
stipulated that any gains made on the money would be split 50-50 with the
trading firm, while any losses would come straight out of his trading account.
"That was actually how a lot of shops operated back then." In that era before
on-line trading, such firms were the only places traders of relatively modest
means could go if they wished to work their own accounts. "A lot of the clients
were retired market makers and options specialists," Velez says. "And of course
individuals who could demonstrate that they had experience with the market
and did relatively well with their own trading. Some firms have as high as a 75
percent payout on your profits. And they also earned money on the
commissions. That's not to say it's entirely bad. That's what gave me and a lot
of traders their starts." Still he says, "It's a very lucrative business." Often it was
lucrative only for the firm.

All the more so, because in addition to commissions, traders also paid interest
on their margin debt, or the money the trading firm advanced them. "My margin
costs would be literally thousands a day," Velez says. "So if I didn't make
anywhere from $5,000 to $10,000 per day, I'd be running against the clock."

Since markets rarely moved with enough volatility to make $5,000 to $10,000
per day, Velez's only recourse was to trade large blocks of shares, thereby
multiplying any fractional moves these stocks made. But imagine the stress if
Velez guessed wrong. By buying on margin he was able to multiply any gains
10-fold. But any losses would likewise be magnified 10 times and would come
directly out of his trading account, along with the commission costs and the
margin payments. One or two trades gone wrong, and he'd be wiped out. The
only way to survive under conditions like that is to thoroughly research your
positions beforehand to convince yourself beyond a shadow of a doubt that you
are correct.

Habits learned during this high-stress trading period have stayed with Velez to
this day.

When I want to buy a stock, size is not an issue, he says. "I want as much as I can get at that price. If I decide to buy, I will throw out an incredibly large flurry of buy orders to take as much stock at that level as I can get."

As a result, he might make anywhere from 40-70 trades per day. "I use the amount of stock that I can get at that level as a barometer for whether or not my analysis is correct," he says. "If I don't get a lot of stock, the odds are I am correct. If I do, the odds are, I am wrong." Of course, he adds – in a don't-try-this-at-home warning – "what I do at my level of trading is different than what I would advise a trader who is not quite there yet."

A traders' dojo

Surprisingly, a lot of the traders who sat near him at the firm were "not quite there yet," despite the fact that they'd spent the bulk of their careers making markets for various securities and derivatives, a job that regularly pitted them against the best and the brightest on Wall Street. Of course as market makers they traded their employers' money. On their own, they often caved under the pressure of losing money that belonged to them. One trader in particular, a former options market maker, was having serious problems, Velez remembers. "He was just hemorrhaging money," says Velez. "This individual couldn't trade his way out of a brown paper bag if it was wet. At this point, I was doing exceptionally well." The man turned to Velez and said, "I never see you upset."

Velez still remembers what he told the man: "If you look around this room," Velez explained, "you see individuals who are being played by the market tick by tick. I reverse it. I play the market. The market doesn't play me. In the quietude of my home in the evening, I come up with 4-5 plays based on my approach. I map out precisely how they will be played: where I will enter and where I will draw the line in the sand. Then I bring this to the market the next day. I set my alerts based on these parameters. And then I read the paper. If the market plays by the rules that I've set up for it the night before, then there's no doubting, there's no hesitation, there's instantaneous action with confidence on a plan that I mapped out the night before."

The options trader thought this was the most profound thing he'd ever heard, Velez recalls. The man asked to see the list of moves Velez had plotted out the night before. Soon all the other 90 traders in the room wanted a crack at Velez's list. And Velez had a secretary at the firm make copies each morning.

A lot of people read a book about price support and resistance. And it makes sense to them. Then they expect to go into the market and play the concept successfully. It doesn't happen that way. The concept has to become yours. It has to become internalized to the point where it's not intellectual. It's in the gut. It's in every fiber of your being.

Velez says that at the same time he was becoming known throughout the New York City area as a successful trader. He began talking to clients at Solomon Smith Barney and to local clubs devoted to using trading software programs like TradeStation (www.tradestation.com) and Metastock (www.metastock.com). By now, hundreds of people were receiving Velez's stock list free by fax each day – until his wife urged him to start charging for it. So Velez tidied up the format. The list featured four daily picks, including detailed instructions on what price to buy and sell – everything you needed in order for the market to come to you. "And that became the Pristine Day Trader," he says, put out by the guy who never seemed to sweat, regardless of what the market did. Day Trader was the tag he put on his pick sheet. But the picks themselves were mainly swing trades. In several months, he says, the Pristine Day Trader became the largest daily advisory service in the nation. And about 90 percent of his clientele was professional.

Buying on dips

Over the years, as online trading became more and more popular, that mix changed. Until today, when about 40 percent of his clients are professional traders. The rest are active traders who work for themselves. To accommodate the expanding base of beginners, he developed seminars on trading fundamentals. Velez's techniques emphasize protecting profits nearly as much as making them. And like his early mentor Dr. Elder, he works on building up confidence in his students. To start off, he advises buying small positions – maybe 200 shares. And as an added precaution he tells his student to never buy a stock unless it's up on the day. Moreover, you should wait till it trades above the previous day's high. Finally, all three broad market averages – the Dow, the S&P, and the NASDAQ – should be trading up on the day as well. "We want to place the beginning trader at risk only when the odds are so overwhelmingly in his favour that he can actually be sloppy and still make money. When students show progress in these environments then we start taking off some of the cuffs." As an example, he'll let a student buy a stock if only two of the three broad market averages are up.

This teaching closely follows Velez's own style of trading, he says. "I am waiting for specific events that have proven me to produce reliable outcomes. When one of these events occur I strike in a very concentrated manner."

One of the events Velez looks for is a short-term retracement – a dip, in other words. It sounds commonsensical. Stocks never march up in price forever. Typically they fall off for several days as groups of traders sell and take their profits. Nevertheless, predicting exactly where a dip will occur takes skill and practice. Velez has developed several techniques. The first uses a simple 50-day moving average. When a stock trading above its moving average begins to decline on light volume, look for it to bounce off the moving average line once again. Then consider buying as the bounce occurs, he'll tell his students. If the upward bounce occurs on heavy volume, so much the better. Very often the stock will rise $2-$3 from there. At that point Velez will often advise people to sell half the original position, to lock in profits. The rest of the position can, one hopes, continue to grow. But it also should be sold in the event it reverses. When you've sold off half a winning position and banked your profits, you should never risk losing that money. Velez says. Therefore, sell the remaining position immediately if it declines to its original purchase price.

Candlestick makers

Using a more advanced tactic, Velez tells students to look for a stock that has just made a new high. If the high is followed by three consecutive down days, look for a reversal. Velez used candlestick charting, a method of technical analysis developed by rice merchants in medieval Japan, to determine the moment when buyers take control of the stock back from sellers. As with some Japanese martial art, you could spend a lifetime delving into the nuances of candlestick charting. Fortunately, popular online charting programs such as eSignal and Window on Wall Street can construct candlestick charts using real-time data automatically. Other services, such as Bigcharts.com, are free but may use delayed data. The charts you create will look more like a series of dark and light dynamite sticks than candlesticks. But an adept reader can discern a pattern and determine how much the price of a stock moved within a given period. A period could be a day, or month, or even five minutes. Equally valuable, you can determine who held the upper hand at the conclusion of each period. If the candlestick is dark, the sellers were in control. Light-colored candlesticks indicate that buyers took control.

Innumerable other candlestick patterns exist and Velez claims that thanks to his years of reading charts he's able to recognize them and act on them almost instinctively. Sitting in a hotel room somewhere awaiting a meeting, he says he can open his laptop, connect to the Internet, quickly get into the "trader's mindset," and then enter the ongoing battle between buyers and sellers.

Oliver Velez's trading rules

- *Minimize market noise by paying close attention to two key indicators: price and volume.*

- *Realize that every moment a stock trades, a battle rages between buyers and sellers.* Each group continuously tries to take control of a stock's momentum from the other.

- *As a beginner, trade small positions.* Before you buy a stock, make sure all three broad market averages are up: the NASDAQ, the S&P, and the Dow.

- *Make sure your average losses are lower than your average gains.* Use tight stops to enforce this rule, even though you risk being stopped out frequently. Never allow yourself to lose more than 10 percent on a stock that trades above $15.

- *Consider selling half the position of a losing trade that's in danger of being stopped out.* Only do this if you strongly believe the stock will rebound shortly.

Chapter Six
On-the-Edge Trading
Barbara Hamilton: Momentum Trader*

"Today was an incredible day," Barbara Hamilton tells me over the phone. "I am extremely happy even as I speak." Hamilton recounts how she'd taken a break from trading and gone to the bank between 3 and 4 o'clock on a February afternoon, braving Boston's blustery winter winds. It was just before the market closed on one of those wild uptrending days that marked the frenetic height of the year 2000 Internet bubble. When she returned and called up her account balance on Quicken.com, she discovered her net worth had risen by $10,000 – in the space of less than one hour. The spike up was mainly thanks to two highly speculative and – at that point in history – expensive stocks: CMGI and ICGE. "Those two have been really plaguing me," Hamilton says.

"They're both Internet incubator companies, I bought CMGI because it was on a roll going up to its split date. And I thought if CMGI goes up, then ICGE is probably going to follow suit. I was completely wrong. ICGE made an announcement that they weren't going to see any earnings for a long, long time, and their stock plunged. I've lost 50 percent on that stock. And I wasn't following my own rule of cutting my losses at 7 percent, which I'm kicking myself for. I see now that it closed up 8 $^{13}/_{16}$. A very welcome sight."

In that quaint, long-gone era before the dot-com stock bubble, only major-league politicians, rock stars, and super-models could make anything close to $10,000 an hour. But throughout the course of '98 and '99, Hamilton would routinely make or lose enough before lunch to buy a nice bungalow in the 'burbs. Her five- and six-figure days were a vivid contrast to her life she'd led before. Back when she was in her twenties, Hamilton, who's now 46, had

---

*At the subject's request, this name is a pseudonym.

focused her considerable creative energies on the classical piano, and she might spend weeks mastering gruelling, complex twentieth-century works. Sadly, it's hard to make a living as a classical pianist. There's just not a lot of turnover among the major symphonies.

> **"In that quaint, long-gone era before the dot-com stock bubble, only major-league politicians, rock stars, and super-models could make anything close to $10,000 an hour. But throughout the course of '98 and '99, Hamilton would routinely make or lose enough before lunch to buy a nice bungalow in the 'burbs. "**

As a result, some years ago, Hamilton opted for a career change and set herself to learning computer programming. "I started out getting involved in networking," she says. "I worked in three different start-up companies. One of them was delivering financial news. I designed their server software. The purpose of it was to deliver news stories to customers on a local area network [LAN]. And I worked in England and designed a gateway that connected to the London Stock Exchange. That was the era of client-server technology, which is somewhat over now."

Throughout that time Hamilton was sort of married into the business, as well. With her help and financial support, she and her husband launched a fledgling computer software business. When the two divorced and the company was sold, Hamilton received her share of the company's sales price. "I was just sitting in the courtroom and they said the amount of money was $525,000, she recalls. "After I got that $525,000, I walked down Newbury Street saying to myself 'I'm rich, I'm rich.' It took a while for me to get used to that idea. I just left the money in my account accumulating 4 percent interest. I was too nervous to do anything with it."

Learning on the job

"In my last job before I quit work to trade, I was the project leader on this team that was responsible for making sure that our 500 worldwide servers were able to function," Hamilton says. "I had hired a co-worker to do some of the Y2K conversion, and I used to go into her office to see what she was doing." Strangely, whenever Hamilton entered the room her co-worker quickly flipped her screen off. "Finally," says Hamilton, "I saw what she'd been so intently focussed on. It was a Datek trading screen. And I said, 'you don't have to stop. Show me what you're doing there.' So she showed me everything."

"That was October '97," Hamilton says. The market was on a roll. Once she'd learned the basics of trading, Hamilton resolved to put her newfound wealth to work. "I had never bought a stock in my life," she says. "It was December 8, 1997. I bought Excite. I remember that was very symbolic. Because it was most exciting." The first trade, like the proverbial first step in a 1,000-mile voyage, is always the hardest. "It was so scary. It is like gambling in the beginning. You don't know what's going to happen. You just type those numbers in. I think I sold my Excite stock two days later and I made $300. I was thrilled. 'This is so easy,' I thought. I was instantly hooked."

> **❝ Unfortunately for the company, my trading really became addictive. My colleague and I were checking prices all the time. ❞**

By the time the New Year rolled around Hamilton had made a decision. She would trade part-time for one year. And if she could make the equivalent of her salary as a software engineer she'd quit her job and ply the markets full-time. Her annual salary at the time was $85,000. Turns out she cleared that much in six months of trading. Even when her day job proved a distraction.

"Unfortunately for the company," she says, "my trading really became addictive. My colleague and I were checking prices all the time." The two were never caught. "I think there were some things that I was late on," she says. "But I don't think they realized why that was happening." People did come by her office, she remembers, with complaints about server crashes and the like. "I thought – yikes – I really should do some work."

But this was an era when you could trade on autopilot and still come out okay. "Cisco was exploding," Hamilton recalls. "I made $9,000 on Cisco in one week. And I didn't check it for two weeks and made thousands more during that time. We thought we were brilliant because it was a serious bull market. What's that famous saying? 'Never mistake a bull market for brains.' My attitude got worse and worse. Money is definitely power in the workplace. You have a different feeling going to work, knowing you have a big fat bank account, than you do if you're $10,000 in debt. Then you're a slave."

High-stakes swing trading

What helped boost Hamilton's gains, no doubt, was that she was able to put a fairly hefty portfolio to work. Stocks at the time were moving up faster than the companies' boards of directors could approve splits. Share prices of $125 or more were common. And so increasingly were stocks selling at $400 or more per share. Fiber optic supplier SDL Inc. (SDLI), one of Hamilton's favourite stocks, might easily rise by $20 or more during intraday trading. To Hamilton, the best possible strategy seemed to be this: use the half-million portfolio to take relatively large positions in a very few expensive stocks. Then sell a few days late when she'd made 10 percent or more – high-stakes swing trading, in effect. A person could make huge amounts in a very short time. Do the math: A 10 percent move on a $400 stock amounts to $40, or $40,000 if you happen to own 1,000 shares. And even a 1- or 2-point gain – something that could transpire over several minutes' time – could bring home a couple thousand.

"I almost always bought stocks all at once," Hamilton recalls. "For a long time, I always bought 1,000 shares at a time, no matter what. But sometimes when I made mistakes, it was just too painful. I kind of lost my confidence. So to get my confidence back, I started buying just 100 shares at a time. So what happened was I bought CMGI at its peak, I bought ICGE at its peak. And when they started going down, I thought, okay, I'm going to average this by buying another 100 shares at a lower price. If it recovers, I'm going to break even at a lower point [by dollar cost averaging or doubling down]. I kept doing this with ICGE. Then the next day is was down another 10 points. And I thought – no problem – I'll buy another 100 shares. And I ended up with 400 shares because four times I had bought it on the way down. And it still hadn't been come close to bottoming out. It went way down from there. So I learned a lesson about that: Don't average on the way down."

Hamilton dabbled in other trading styles besides swing trading. "I did real day trading," she says. As a day trader, she focused on a single stock: Dell Computer (DELL), buying and selling it several times over the course of a day. "It really got stressful," Hamilton remembers. "Because you can't tell from one moment to the next whether it's going up or down. But I was using a kind of timing method, where if things shot up at the beginning of the day, quite often the highest price of the day is about 10 o'clock. And then the market starts to cool down and reach a low around 10:30. You see the price going down." Then Hamilton says, she looked for a big buy order – something on the order of 5,000 or 10,000 shares – her assumption being that someone at a mutual fund or institution had sniffed a bottom. "So that's an indication to buy. Buy on a big buy," she says. To find out whether a large order was an offer to buy or sell, she studied the 3D Stock Charts feature you link to at the Web site of the electronic communications network Island.com. 3D Stock Charts depicts buy-side orders in green. Red bars indicate sell limit orders.

> **❝** The problem with day trading is that you can only do one stock at a time when you're watching minute by minute. **❞**

Despite some successes, Hamilton said she gave up on day trading. "The problem with day trading is that you can only do one stock at a time when you're watching minute by minute." Track more than that and your attention's bound to wander. "My account was too big," she says. "I could buy 1,000 shares of Dell. But the rest of my money would just be sitting there."

So why not day trade one stock and devote the rest of her portfolio to swing trading? Hamilton says that didn't work for her either. "It gets confusing when you mix strategies. Let's say I did 80 percent of my portfolio on momentum (swing) trading and 20 percent on day trading. It's all I can do to keep track of my momentum plays right now."

The $359,000 bet

One reason Hamilton decided she needed to focus strictly on momentum or swing trading: "My income from month to month was unbelievably erratic, because I was trying different methods," she says. In January 1999, for example, Hamilton made $124,000. That was because she had been lucky enough to buy a basketful of stocks during a market dip in December. "It just so happened that December 11 was the bottom," she says. "And in January everything exploded." In February '99 Hamilton figures she made about $16,000. In March, her earnings more than doubled to $33,000. And in April – even as investors fretted over whether Y2K would bring about the collapse of civilization or worse – Hamilton raked in $144,000.

"I used one technique that succeeded brilliantly." Like another trade profiled in this book, Bob Martin, Hamilton decided to follow the advice of Internet stock guru Steve Harmon. "He was compiling this thing called the IPOdex," Hamilton remembers. In essence this was an index of hot recently IPOed Internet companies. "I selected about eight of those companies that I thought were the best," says Hamilton. "And I just started tracking them in a Quicken portfolio, pretending that I had bought 100 shares of each on a day when I thought they were all too high to buy. I was testing my own theory that I thought they were too high. But it turned out that if I had bought them that day, I would have made a lot of money. So I watched the 100 shares of each of those stocks. And in late April '99 the NASDAQ dropped. I still didn't own any of the stocks from Harmon's list at that point. I wasn't sure what was going on," she says. Nor was she sure if the drop was a momentary blip or the beginning of a long-term downward trend. "The next day I watched until the market started to recover. I think it recovered about 15 percent. And I thought, 'Okay, that shows that it's on its way back.'" So Hamilton began buying heavily.

The stocks she bought included all the household-names, Internet-wunderkind firms, companies that were likewise mainstays in the portfolios of thousands of tech-hungry investors. Among her buys: e-business application software provider Vignette Corp. (VIGN), business-to-business Web site builder VerticalNet (VERT), the online computer content provider CNET, along with CMGI, Yahoo (YHOO), and America Online (AOL).

"This was a big risk," she recalls, "because I committed about $359,00 out of a total account of $500,000 to that trade." Perhaps because she was nervous, Hamilton ended up selling some of her positions the very next day. She sold off a few more a week later. "By April 27, I had made $94,000." And that was just on those seven stocks. "It made me feel like this is insane. I just didn't believe that I could pull it off. I was working my way up to that million-dollar point. I was very close to it at that time. I suddenly started thinking, 'Aah ... I'm going to buy a condominium on the waterfront. I could buy a Jaguar!"

Wisely, as it turned out she ended up buying a Honda Accord.

Millionaires don't buy their own grapefruit

By any accounts, the money was flowing in during a markedly bizarre period for the markets. "Every day it was just going up, going up. And I was making more and more profit," Hamilton recalls. "I thought at some point I'm going to just cash in on this whole thing, because this is too good to be true. And on the morning of April 27 the futures were down, and a few things started to drop." Some of the stocks Hamilton owned had gapped down when they opened. "Within 15 minutes I sold everything I had," she says. "Later on in the day, I did a calculation where I made $94,000 on that day. If I had waited until noon, I would have made $63,000."

How did that make her feel? "I thought that I just deposited $94,000 in this account. I've got to tell somebody." Hamilton decided she'd rush out to visit a friend, Paula, who also traded stocks out of her home. Paula and Hamilton often conversed via phone or e-mail, getting each other's take on the market. But Hamilton wanted to relay this news in person. "I was looking for where my car was parked. I went to the garage. I went back to the street. Then I realized that the city of Boston had towed my car. And I thought – so what I'll just buy another one. That was a great moment. So I just took a cab to visit my friend."

On May 6, thanks to another flurry of successful trades, Hamilton's account topped a million bucks. She marked the fact on her calendar with the word *Million* in pencil. But instead of feeling ecstatic as she had when she'd cashed out her last basket of stocks for a $94,000 profit, this time it all felt kind of creepy. "I didn't want to tell anybody," Hamilton says. "I thought people would start treating me differently. My friends would think that I might not want to be friends with them any more. And I felt sort of fearful. I thought 'Watch, I'll be hit by a car. Watch, I'll find out I have cancer.' It's like this feeling that now I really have something to lose. So it would be so tragic if something happened."

She was all by herself at the time. "I kept thinking of it all day. I was standing in the fruit aisle, thinking 'I'm a millionaire.' And I'm looking at these grapefruits. And I thought, 'I've looked at them many times before, but I was never a millionaire before.' I questioned everything I was doing, I thought, 'Wow, why don't I have somebody else buy my grapefruit for me?' And I was driving, and I thought maybe I shouldn't be driving. I should be having someone else drive me. My ex-husband called me that day. I hadn't talked to him in a long time. He just called to see how I was doing. I said, 'Great, I just made a million dollars!' He was the only person I told. It was a beautiful day."

The higher they fly . . .

Remember, this was in May '99. The bull market still had nine months of steam left. And the final surge would bring even more outrageous profits to traders like Hamilton. But the ride would be far from smooth. Hamilton had amassed an arsenal of techniques that had served her well so far. For starters, she considered herself a decent market timer. Plus, she says, she knew a few stocks well enough to recognize some good buying opportunities.

"I usually only have about four to six positions." Tracking more had proved simply too much of a hassle. "I try to buy stocks that are well known, that are running on some upward momentum." Momentum might come from stock splits, whether officially announced or rumored. Hamilton pays frequent visits to a Web site called SplitTrader.com, that e-mails news about splits.

Abnormal volume can also signal momentum. Web sites such as FreeRealTime.com routinely list the day's high-volume moves. But, she says, an even simpler, if less exact way, to gauge interest in a stock is to watch how often it appears on the scrolling ticker continually displayed on CNBC.

To find stocks, she often relied on the daily screens printed in *Investors Business Daily*. Her rule was to choose only stocks with a 99 99 AAA rating, the highest possible. The first 99 refers to earnings per share, and it indicated that the company is in the 99th percentile in terms of earnings growth. The second 99 denotes a stock's relative strength, and also places the company in the 99th percentile for that indicator. The first *A* means the stock is being accumulated aggressively. By contrast, a *C* would be a neutral rating and a *D* or *E*

> **❝ I told myself, 'Back off.' But I just couldn't do it. This was truly an example of addiction, I believe. Because it was so thrilling to watch those stocks going up, I just wanted to experience it again. ❞**

would indicate the stock was being distributed, meaning its prices would likely decline over the near term. The second *A* signifies that well-performing mutual funds have sizable positions in the stock. Since those funds are performing well, so the reasoning goes, they would have little reason to sell. And the third *A* means that the stock's sector is outperforming the market as a whole.

But as May progressed, something changed. "I was watching the market close enough that I knew it was going to start heading down," she says. "It had just gone up so high that it had to have a pullback period. I thought the pullback would come in May. So I told myself, 'Back off.' But I just couldn't do it. This was truly an example of addiction, I believe. Because it was so thrilling to watch those stocks going up, I just wanted to experience it again. And I bought a few thousand shares on May 10. This was how I lost my million. I kept buying more stock, even though I thought it was going to go down. And suddenly I lost $12,000 on something called Cyberian Outpost. And I lost a bunch of money on some other stocks. It was all psychological. I just couldn't admit that I had lost that money. And that's when I started to realize that if you own a stock and it goes down by a huge amount, you actually have lost that amount of money. Because you could sell the stock that day and you could buy another stock, and it could go up faster than the first stock will recover.

"All of June, July, and August, the market kept going down. My account was minus $25,000 then it was minus $50,000, then it was minus $90,000. And it was getting scarier. During the month of August I didn't do a single trade." Nor did she trade in September. Instead she held on, either out of hope or denial.

"My worst point that I reached was minus $295,000. Which was just about everything I gained. It was just mind-numbing. It was like I was frozen. I was so horrified that this had happened. It all happened so gradually. I thought I lost so much, I'll just wait and see if it turns around. And then it would go down some more. This weird psychology that prevents you from acting: I got really depressed about it. I kind of went into hibernation. I never did get that $1-million condominium on the waterfront."

Eventually, in October, she did sell off her losing positions, just as the market was poised for a recovery. There would be good times again, through the fall and winter of 1999-2000, days when she might make $30,000 or more. But then would come the crash, and it would sorely hurt her. As markets tumbled several hundred points in the course of a day, her own daily losses might amount to nearly $100,000. Those same stocks that had climbed by $40 or even $100 in a day were now suddenly evaporating before the eyes of investors. When we last spoke by phone, Hamilton was still trading. And she was bound and determined to make back her million.

Barbara Hamilton's trading rules

- *Only trade stocks with average daily volume above 1,000,000.*

- *When studying charts, start by looking at the one-year chart, then gradually zoom in.* Looking at six-month, three-month, one-month, one-week, then intraday charts. Note any relationships between volume and price movements at each point.

- *Have a strategy for each stock.* Write that strategy down when you buy the stock. Clearly specify under what circumstances you will exit the stock and under what circumstances you'll hold it.

- *Sell a stock after it's gone down 7-10 percent.*

- *If things look too good to be true cash out.*

- *Buy on a big buy.* If a stock's been drifted downward, a large purchase may indicate that an institutional buyer has sensed a bottom.

- *Don't average down.* Accept losses and move on.

- *Hold four to six large positions, and trade them intensely.*

Chapter Seven
Pennies from Heaven
Chris Farrell: The Scalper

If you're a football fan, maybe you remember Super Bowl XXV back in 1991. The game pitted the New York Giants against the highly favoured Buffalo Bills. Yet the Giants won it 20–19 – even though they were clearly outclassed, and they knew it. To compensate, the Giants played an exceedingly methodical game that focused on maintaining possession of the ball and running out the clock. With each play, the team painstakingly eked out 3- and 4-yard running gains on a long relentless march toward the goal line.

Chris Farrell, 27, author of *The Day Trader's Survival Guide* likes to compare his own trading strategy to that now-famous championship. He's well aware that he is hopelessly outgunned by the Street's professional traders. But he can still beat them at their own game. His is a trading strategy built on $\frac{1}{16}$-of-a-point gains, which in traders's parlance makes him a scalper or a grinder. Not exactly flattering terms. But maybe that's because many day traders would rather take far bigger risks and reach for that one great trade – the one that'll bring them over the top – whereas Farrell would rather build up his account tiny piece by tiny piece, while keeping his risks to an absolute minimum.

A little math reveals how it works: If Farrell makes $\frac{1}{16}$ of a point on a 2,000-share trade, he will net about $125 ($105 after commissions). Do a half-dozen successful trades like that each day, and you can easily pay the rent. "The strategies that I recommend are not going to take in the kind of money you could realize by taking more risk as a momentum trader," he says. "I have a lot of friends who are momentum traders, and they make more money in seven or eight months than I've made in my entire life. But those are not the kind of strategies that I feel comfortable with."

Of course Farrell's being a little modest here. During his career of roughly five years, he estimates he's taken well over seven figures from the market. In a good month, he says he can earn $40,000 just from trading his own account.

He also uses the money in his own account to pay the bills, which can be sizable in Manhattan, where he makes his home. "I withdraw money to meet expenses," he says. "That's a psychological problem in itself. Because obviously your goal is to have your account grow. It's painful to pull money out to meet expenses. It plays with your mind. It's not like with someone else where you get a paycheck and you feel like – yeah – I earned it, and you take the money home. In this case, you feel like you're taking something away from your hard-earned money."

In addition to his own account, Farrell also manages a small hedge fund, using the same scalping strategy. He started the fund with contributions from family members and associates. And although he won't disclose the amount of the fund's assets, he says returns have averaged better than 50 percent over the years. Those $1/16$-point gains add up.

"It's steady money," he says. "You don't really have too many big swings. You grind it out. Big one-day gains come from a lot of trades. They don't come from one large position of 5,000 shares that makes you 1 or 2 points. It comes from turning the account over and maybe making 60 or 70 trades on it of 2,000- to 5,000-share lots and just banging it out that way. If a stock tends to be particularly active, I may be in and out of the same issue 15 or 20 times a day."

To repeat, that's 15 or 20 round-trip trades centered on a single stock. On any given day Farrell may have positions in anywhere from four to 12 different stocks. He estimates that in the course of each day he moves $1.5 million into and out of the market. Which means that in a year's time he channels hundreds of millions through the market

"I have a lot of friends who are momentum traders, and they make more money in seven or eight months than I've made in my entire life. But those are not the kind of strategies that I feel comfortable with. "

– as much as many large mutual fund managers. Or viewed another way, he moves the same few hundred thousand into and out of the market untold thousands of times.

In praise of boring stocks

Many would question why Farrell would settle for a mere 6 cents a share (roughly $\frac{1}{16}$ of a point) when other successful traders ride their shares up by several dollars or more. Cut your winners short and let your winners run, as the saying goes. And after all, that's what the momentum stocks day traders love tend to do. They move $3, $6 or $8 per day. But you have to understand how Farrell's strategy is unique.

> **❝ The stocks Farrell trades rarely budge more than $\frac{1}{8}$ or $\frac{1}{4}$ of a point on any given day. To most traders these are incredibly boring stocks. But that's just how Farrell likes them. ❞**

Most people think of scalpers as hyperactive opportunists in need of Ritalin. These scalpers, according to the image, will fly in and out of NASDAQ momentum stocks. And indeed, these stocks can move $\frac{11}{16}$ of a point with each tick, as millions of shares get passed from one momentum trader to another. Farrell does a certain amount of momentum trading, to be sure. However, when practicing the scalping strategy that is his bread and butter he only trades New York Stock Exchange (NYSE) stocks. What's more, the stocks Farrell trades rarely budge more than $\frac{1}{8}$ or $\frac{1}{4}$ of a point on any given day. To most traders these are incredibly boring stocks. But that's just how Farrell likes them.

Boring stocks trade on low volume – from 20,000 to 50,000 shares daily. By contrast, Cisco's (CSCO) average daily volume is just shy of 35 million shares. Often, as you'll see, the boring stocks Farrell likes are oblivious to the market turmoil around them. For that reason, Farrell can swoop into a boring stock and carve out a profit from the tiniest of spreads – usually when no one is looking.

To really understand how Farrell's scalping strategy works, you first need to know a little bit about the differences in the way stocks trade on the NASDAQ and the NYSE, and consequently why Farrell's scalping tactics work only on the NYSE.

The NASDAQ, of course is favored by the great majority of active traders. And one of the reasons – as you'll see in a moment – is that the exchange uses a system of market makers who act as middlemen by taking the other side of people's trades. Think of market makers as day traders themselves. Only instead of using their own capital, they have the backing of mega-trading firms such as Merrill Lynch or Goldman Sachs. When you enter an order to buy or sell a stock at its market price (a market order), your online broker normally routes that order directly to a particular market maker. And it's the market maker who takes the other side of your trade. Nobody likes a middleman cutting into his or her profits. But market makers help keep the NASDAQ running smoothly. They ensure that there will always be a buyer if you are the seller and a seller if you are the buyer.

Market makers often compete with each other as well as with the day traders. You can watch this jousting if you have trading software that includes a Level II screen. Traders like the fact that they can route orders to any number of competing market makers or fellow traders. They have options.

The NYSE is organized in a very different manner. And consequently for traders, the options are seemingly far more limited. Instead of enlisting the help of several competing market makers to trade particular stocks, the NYSE uses a single middleman called a "specialist". The specialist is obligated to ensure that an orderly market exists for the stock he or she happens to be representing. To do that the specialist agrees to be the buyer and seller of last resort. That means that whenever you want to sell a stock you can be assured that someone is on hand to buy it. The price may not be what you want to pay. But a buyer will be there. Same goes if you wish to buy stock. Like market makers, specialists make their money from the spread, that is, the difference between the bid and the ask price. However, the specialist's obligation to maintain an orderly market means they must maintain a reasonable spread.

The world inside the spread

End of background lesson. Here's how Farrell makes his money: by getting inside this spread. Let's say the bid on a stock is 10 and the ask is 10 $3/16$. Farrell might place his bid for 2,000 shares at 10$1/16$. Then he simply waits. The next time someone enters a market order to sell 2,000 shares or a lesser amount Farrell is pretty certain he'll be the one buying those shares. How can he be so sure that he'll receive the shares? Farrell explains that his strategy profits from a particular NYSE rule. To wit: The specialist has to put a customer's orders ahead of his own. For Farrell that means as long as his is the high bid, he'll get the shares.

> I don't really feel comfortable holding anything longer than overnight, because I feel like that's a bet outside the parameters of supply and demand. And for me that borders on gambling.

Once Farrell gets the shares, he can immediately turn around and sell them for 10 ⅛. Again, this puts him first in line on the ask side of the spread. So when a buyer comes along with a market order for 2,000 shares, Farrell is the one doing the selling.

Does it always work out that easily? Hardly. Farrell says only one in three of his orders to buy or sell stock actually get filled. When buy orders don't get filled, it's no big deal. But holding on to a 2,000-share position can be risky if you live and die by tiny fractions. So occasionally Farrell allows that he has to be patient and keep his order in place until the market comes to him. Nevertheless, he claims a 90 percent success rate with his scalping trades. "But the profit margins have been razor thin: ¹/₁₆ and ⅛," he says. "On the losing trades I try to keep those losses the same."

Market exotica

Wait a minute, you say, why wouldn't these stocks move up and down in price, the way stocks do, and quickly evaporate those ¹/₁₆-point gains? With most stocks, that might certainly be the case. But remember, Farrell's strategy depends on his trading stocks that rarely move at all. Many of these stocks – *financial instruments* would be a better name – are completely unknown to the average investor.

"On the NYSE most of the low volatility stocks are interest-rate plays. They're not equity plays," he explains. He's talking first about *preferred stocks*, which differ from *common shares* in two key ways: (1) They pay a fixed dividend, just like a bond. (2) Often the dividend rate is adjusted automatically based on some interest–rate benchmark. In other words, preferreds behave much like bonds, but with maybe more liquidity. Like bonds they are highly interest-rate sensitive. "You could find preferreds that may yield in the range of 8 percent," Farrell says. "So when you have a serious back-up (rise) in interest rates, the trading volume can trail off significantly. When rates stop rising, the volume seems to flood back in. And it becomes easy money on that down cycle."

Another type of financial instrument Farrell likes to trade, because it rarely budges most trading days, is so-called debt hybrids. These are similar to closed-end bond funds because they may bundle several debt instruments together.

Quick review: A closed-end fund, remember, is a mutual fund that's diced up into a finite number of shares. These shares trade like a stock. In the case of a closed-end bond fund, the manager might purchase a series of bonds of, say, a particular grade or from a particular company or industry. To illustrate with a highly simplified example: If the total assets of the fund were $10 million, and the fund managers divided up that amount into 10,000 shares, each share would then be worth $1,000 to start. But from then on, its price would move up and down just like a stock depending on the interest rate climate at that particular moment.

"A lot of debt hybrids are of the highest credit quality," says Farrell. "That's in essence a triple-A rated security. So you're not going to have any volatility. I remember 2 or 3 years ago, the Dow was down 500 points in one day. Those things weren't even budging an inch. That's why I feel comfortable with a 2,000- to 5,000-share position."

The hard part isn't so much trading debt hybrids. It's finding them. "Unfortunately there seems to be a complete lack of information on debt hybrids," says Farrell. "The newspapers aren't even reliable. I've come across issues that trade in the range of 20,000 shares. Sometimes you check in the newspapers and you don't even see the closing price. It's even harder to see symbols on them. It's not a mainstream product."

A good broker can locate some viable candidates, however. Popular bond trading Web sites such as Bondsonline (www.bondsonline.com), ConvertBond.com (www.convertbond.com), and Investing in Bonds (www.investinginbonds.com) may also point you in the right direction. In the past, Farrell has traded debt hybrid products issued by utility companies. And he has been particularly fond of products issued by the quasi-private Southern utility, The Tennessee Valley Authority.

Preferred stocks are somewhat easier to locate. Just enter the name of a company in the stock symbol look-up area of Quicken.com (www.quicken.com) and you'll come up with a list of all the classes of stocks issued by that company. To broaden your search enter the name of, say, a publicly traded utility stock at Quicken and you can use that site's comparison feature to find similar stocks.

An insider's advantage

Farrell figures there are several hundred financial instruments trading on the NYSE that would be workable using his strategy. It's worth noting that this number is roughly comparable to the number of high profile, epileptic tech stocks that hoards of momentum traders eagerly leap into each day. However,

Farrell and those day traders who use methods similar to his – a relatively small group – have their boring stocks largely to themselves.

It's also worth noting that Farrell – thanks to his background – had a somewhat easy time locating the stocks he trades. After graduating from Colgate University, Farrell took a job with Olde, the discount broker in Detroit. He spent six months there, working at their preferred-stock trading desk. Wanting to move closer to his friends on the East Coast, he accepted a similar job at the trading desk at Gruntal an investment advisory firm based in New York. Both the Olde job and the one at Gruntal required Farrell to trade very much like a market maker or specialist. If a customer – be it an individual or an institution – wanted 1,000 shares of XYZ preferred stock, Farrell might borrow the shares from one of the firm's other clients and deliver them to the customer requesting the shares. In effect, he was acting as a trader and selling the stock short, a common practice. The transaction would go through at the same ask price quoted on the NYSE. Then, if later that day another customer wanted to sell 1,000 shares of XYZ Farrell could cover his short position and purchase the shares – only this time he would buy them at the current best bid price. In that way, Farrell's firm profited from the spread the same way a NYSE specialist might. And of course he would only enter the trade on behalf of the firm if he were reasonably certain he could exit profitably.

"There's some risk in that," Farrell says. "You're providing liquidity to a customer, where there may not be liquidity in the market. Let's say that on the floor of the exchange there were only 100 shares for sale, and an order to buy 5,000 shares came across our trading desk. The firm would put its own capital at risk. And we would fill the entire order to the customer at the asking price. And obviously we would go into the market and try to make a profit on it by covering. We'd make eighths, quarters, that kind of thing.

"If I have a customer order coming in for 5,000 shares, where I fill him is dependent on how big the bid and ask sizes are on the NYSE at the time." For example, he explains, "If the stock was trading on a ⅛-point spread, I would be very reluctant to short the stock and fill him on the entire order if there were 10,000 shares on the bid. Because that indicates that there are other buyers out there. And you could get yourself into a short squeeze situation. It's not stocks dropping that typically causes you to lose money as a market maker. Many times it's filling the demand that you have in house (by selling the stock short) and then being unable to cover your position in the market."

Farrell also traded against the market and built up the firm's inventory of a stock if an opportunity arose. "If you spot value in the market," he explains, "you go in and you buy a large block. And then feed it out to the sales force. Again, you'd buy it on the bid and sell it on the ask."

Thinking back, Farrell says he liked the performance-driven atmosphere of Gruntal's trading desk, the "sense of immediate gratification and immediate loss," as he puts it. "There's no office politics in trading rooms. It's a true meritocracy. You are getting precisely what you put in." His stints at Olde and Gruntal also taught him the stealthy tactics professional traders use to sweep $1/16$ and $1/32$ from the market. And it convinced him such a strategy was profitable. Why else would every major trading firm maintain a trading desk of their own? Most important, Farrell realized that he could make more money trading his own account using the very same arcane financial instruments he was currently trading, namely debt hybrids and preferreds.

The cloaking device

Part of the key to perfecting his strategy lay in understanding precisely how specialists operate. This was especially critical given the screen specialists are allowed to operate behind.

"The NYSE is a more fair and more orderly market than the NASDAQ," says Farrell. "But the one flaw it does have is that it doesn't allow the individual to see the order book. If you see someone bidding for 100 shares you don't even know if it is the specialist or not." Even more important, says Farrell, "if that someone is bidding for 100 shares at 40, no one other than the specialist knows how many buyers there are that are below the market. Is there a buyer for 100,000 shares at $39^7/_8$? Or are there no buyers at $39^7/_8$? Maybe the next buyer's down at $39^1/_2$. That kind of information influences trading decisions," he says. By contrast, the NASDAQ order book will display not only the top bid and ask price, but the list of competing bids that are just off those high prices. (For a discussion of how the NASDAQ Level II order book works, see page 11). But with NYSE stocks all you see is the current bid and ask along with the size of each – and also in some cases the size of the last trade. "That's why I go with illiquid, slower moving, less volatile stocks," says Farrell. When there are few buyers and sellers, there's not a lot of information the specialist can hide, he explains. "I in essence neutralize the trading advantage that the specialist has over me."

That's not to say Farrell's strategy is risk-free. "If you're on top of the ask by $1/16$, someone might jump ahead of you and others will follow and in that way drive down the price of the stock," he says. The $1/16$-point gain you were hoping to get could quickly turn into a loss of ⅛ of a point or more – which could in turn melt away a day's worth of previous gains. But once more, because the stocks Farrell chooses trade on such low volume, volatile price run-downs rarely occur.

When Farrell is caught holding shares, he'll resort to any of several tactics. For example, it's common for Farrell to hold positions overnight, betting that the stock's low volatility will bring the price back to his entry level as trading calms down the next day. Farrell also might revert to the old gambler's trick of "doubling down" on his closing position, to reduce the average cost basis in his stock. But this strategy can backfire. Farrell has wound up owning thousands of shares of a stock that's failed to reverse sufficiently to allow him a profitable exit. On occasion he's held more shares than the amount traded on a given day. Selling the shares in one huge order would drive the price down further, of course. So instead Farrell uses a technique employed by specialists and market makers. That is he sells the stock off gradually, 100 or 500 shares at a time. Sometimes unloading a stock in this way can take up to two weeks.

Trading against the house and with it

A far bigger risk occurs when the specialist catches him in the act, so to speak. As a scalper, Farrell tries to scrape profits off the plate of the specialist. His gain is their loss. Furthermore, with illiquid stocks there aren't that many crumbs to go around. "The problem is that the specialist will trade around you," says Farrell. Typically he'll know you're a speculator if you've been in the stock more than once in that day. If he just filled you on 2,000 shares offered, he's going to know."

As Farrell explains it, "Specialists can trade around you essentially by giving what's called 'price improvement.' Let's say there was a wide spread – $9^{15}/_{16}$ to $10^{1}/_{8}$. I went in there and I bid 10. And I was lucky enough to get filled. Then, I go in there and sell at $10^{1}/_{16}$. That means $10^{1}/_{16}$ becomes my offer." Farrell is offering to sell his stock at the lowest current market price, in other words. The next market buy order that comes along, the stock will trade at $10^{1}/_{16}$, and I will be the seller. But the specialist is at his discretion. If he wants he can sell form his own account at 10. And a lot of times that means he's not making any money. He's just doing it to get rid of me."

Another slightly more complicated situation arises when the specialist attempts to masquerade as an investor in an effort to squash speculators like Farrell. "If I see a bid for 5,000 shares, I assume it's not the specialist but another investor.

Because there's no reason for the specialist to show 5,000 shares," he explains. By offering to buy 5,000 shares, the specialist will almost certainly drive the price of the stock up. For that reason, says Farrell the specialist will normally show only 500 shares, especially if the stock trades on low volume. "But every once in a while you'll see 5,000 shares," says Farrell. The large size of the order might convince Farrell that some institution was intent on acquiring the stock, for example. And because of that, Farrell's liable to be fooled into thinking the stock's price would continue to rise. And he could expect to profit nicely. But Farrell's liable to be fooled into thinking the stock's price would continue to rise. And he could expect to profit nicely. But Farrell's been around the block, of course. So to be safe, he says, "I will put a bid in behind the 5,000 share order." That is, his bid will be at a slightly lower price than the bid for the 5,000 shares. "I will think that I am at the end of the line. When in fact there is no line." In other words, Farrell will

> **" There's kind of a weird thing that can't be quantified, I call it 'the temperament of the specialist.' Different stocks are more favorable to this strategy than others. As a novice you may spend a month or two kind of feeling it out. "**

offer to buy the stock at fractionally lower price. Then the specialist might conceivably withdraw the bid for 5,000 shares and hit Farrell's bid. Farrell might not be able to sell the stock profitably. The situation would have been even worse had Farrell placed his bid ahead of the 5,000 share bid. Just as you can grow rich from $1/16$, you can also go broke.

Fortunately, not all specialists are hell-bent on wiping out their competition. "There's kind of a weird thing that can't be quantified," Farrell says. "I call it 'the temperament of the specialist.' Different stocks are more favorable to this strategy than others. As a novice you may spend a month or two kind of feeling it out. I have a lot of bread and butter names that seem to be more receptive than others."

Sometimes the specialist can actually help out a scalper like Farrell. Let's go back to the example where XYZ stock has a spread of $9^{15}/_{16}$ to $10^{1}/_{8}$. Farrell puts in a bid to buy it at 10. "If a block of stock comes in for sale that's larger than my bid for 2,000 shares," he explains, "many times what the specialist will do is pair my order with his own at an even lower price and fill me. Let's say 5,000 shares come in for sale, I'm willing to buy 2,000 shares for 10. What the specialist will do is take that 5,000 share sell order. I want 2,000. The specialist will buy the other 3,000. Well, once the specialist is involved like that the trade's not going to occur at 10: it will probably occur at a lower price like 9 $^{15}/_{16}$ or 9 $^{7}/_{8}$. So essentially you are participating with the specialist in getting a better execution than you would have ordinarily gotten. He will only do that for you because he is obligated to. It's not going to happen typically unless he's wanting to buy stock himself."

Low-tech brokers

For Farrell, the daily dramas of jousting and sometimes cooperating with NYSE specialists occur right in his Manhattan apartment on a single HPO Pavilion computer. Farrell uses a real-time quote system called DTNIQ (www.interquote.com), which costs him about $80 per month. "For this kind of strategy you need bid and ask and you need bid size and ask size," he says. "And if you have a function called 'time and sales,' that also helps because it shows where the prints have been that day. If you're trading illiquid stocks that only trade 40,000 shares in a day, you can get a pretty good feel from those prints where the stock's been trading. If the majority of the volume has been at $10^{1}/_{16}$ and 10, I like my chances of being able to buy it at 10 and sell it at $10^{1}/_{16}$, simply because those prints have already occurred during the day. But if the highest trade of the day has been at 10, and no trades have occurred at $10^{1}/_{16}$, I will be less likely to buy at 10. Because I won't be able to get an execution at $10^{1}/_{16}$."

You might think that because Farrell operates as a scalper he would require a turbo-charged direct access broker – one that would give him ultra-fast executions. In fact just the opposite is true. "Because of the rules of the NYSE, you can get away with using a regular online broker to execute your trades," he says. "In essence you are exploiting the online brokers. Because they don't want to have too many customers like me using limit orders. They would rather have customers trading at market so their market makers could make money by making the spread. In this case you're only paying [Brown & CO] $10 for a limit order. So for a 5,000-share trade, your per-share costs are minimal. So you can sit there all day and make $^{1}/_{16}$. With a direct access trading system that uses Super Dot (the electronic trading network used by the NYSE), you might pay 2 cents per share to get in and 2 cents to get out. You could no longer use this strategy because you'd be paying your entire profit margins in commission. Online brokers are obligated to use the same order-handling rules as the NYSE. So when my bid goes to my online broker, either they take the other side of the trade or they have to send it down to the post of the specialist. And what that does is in essence getting floor access for a much cheaper price."

Of course, it doesn't always work that easily. "Sometimes with the more illiquid stocks," Farrell says, "online brokers themselves will play games with an order and they will route it to third-party exchanges like regional exchanges. That doesn't serve a customer like me well, because you want to make sure that you get to the NYSE floor to help ensure that you get a cleaner execution."

The daily grind

Farrell's strategy may present problems to beginners. It's difficult to practice by paper trading because you can't be sure of the executions you'll get. (Remember Farrell's own estimate that only one in three of his orders actually gets filled.) Furthermore, his strategy depends on locating stocks that barely budge in the course of the day. Farrell's first book, *Day Trade Online* contains a list of candidates that might fit the bill. Most are hardly household names. Examples include: El Paso Electric (EE) Central Vermont Public Service Corp (CV), and Washington Real Estate Investment Trust (WRE). He's also building a Web site, Farrell Trading (www.farrelltrading.com), where traders can discuss additional candidates.

Farrell advises beginners to create a watch list of slow moving, boring stocks, and then continually cull out those stocks that routinely move up or down by more than $1/2$ point intraday. Another possible watch list might be made up of boring stocks that have spreads wider than $1/8$ of a point. He warns that wide spreads are either indicative of volatility or an invitation for other traders to move in and eke out profits for themselves. In other words, don't expect the wide spreads to last very long.

But what's liable to happen to the already razor-thin spread once decimalization takes hold? Farrell insists he'll still be able to work his strategy. When he traded at Gruntal the spreads were $1/8$-point wide, he says. "When those spreads moved from $1/8$ to $1/16$, there was still a ton of opportunity out there. I tend to think that the spread will not narrow much more. Because if it does narrow more, if it moves from 6 cents down to 3 cents, it's going to reach a natural point where the profit margins for someone like me are not going to be there any more. So we would not even trade these stocks. And the spreads would widen back up again."

Maybe the biggest danger of his strategy, he admits, is that trading boring stocks can become – well – boring. Boredom can lead to complacency, which can lead to carelessness and to losses. And losses easily mount up when your strategy depends on the tiniest of gains. Farrell combats trading fatigue by occasionally dabbling in NASDAQ stocks. He's also written his two books while scraping endless $\frac{1}{16}$-point profits from the market. And he finds time to plan a video on trading and to teach seminars. "This kind of scalping strategy doesn't force you to be glued to the screen all day," he says. "It's a lot more strategic, but not as gut wrenching." On any particular day, he says one stock might be very good to trade. "You might be in and out of that issue five times. And then for the rest of the week it could be dead. It's an entirely different animal than what a lot of momentum traders are used to."

Well, maybe a little boredom is just what many of us need.

Chris Farrells's trading rules*

- *Realize the inherent conflict of interest that exists between Wall Street firms and their clients.* While advising you to buy or sell, they take the other side of your trade and make a tiny profit each time from the spread.

- *Remember there are only a limited number of shares available at a given price.* Once those shares change hands, the prevailing price of the stock will change.

- *Trade like a market maker.* That is, think of yourself as the middleman in the market. Like any middleman, you shouldn't be concerned with the longer-term direction of the market. Instead focus on the spread that confronts you at any given moment.

- *Trade "boring stocks."* That is, stocks that typically trade within a very narrow range on volume of between 20,000 and 80,000 shares. The most stable stocks tend to be preferreds, closed-end bond funds, and so-called debt hybrids. Because such stocks trade within a highly predictable range, you have more assurance that you'll be able to exit a position at an acceptable price.

- *Trade using a normal online broker as opposed to a direct access broker.* Online brokers are obligated to route limit orders they don't fill themselves directly to the exchange, but don't charge the access fees to use Super Dot nor the high commissions direct access brokers charge.

---

*These rules apply mainly to the scalping strategy outlined in this chapter, which involves trading NYSE stocks.

- *Ignore charts of any kind and instead focus on the simple quote display that details the spread,* the size of the order on the bid and ask, and the amount of last sale. As an option use a quote service that provides a time-of-sale figure showing "prints" of all the bids and asks over the course of the trading day. This allows you to see not only the trading range but also the size of the spread, which is useful in judging optimal entry and exit points.

- *Accept the fact that only one out of three of your orders will end up being filled.*

- *The more liquid the stock, the higher the trading advantage the specialist has over you.* This is because only the specialist can see all the backed up offers to buy and sell stock on his order book.

- *Trade in and out of a variety of stocks over the course of the day so the specialists handling those stocks aren't aware of your presence.*

- *If you get stuck in a position as the price moves against you, unload the stock gradually over the course of days.* As an alternative, more experienced traders might consider averaging down.

- *Trade 2,000-share lots, since a larger amount would create a buying imbalance in low volume stocks.* A $1/16$ point gain on a 2,000-share lot equals $125. Four successful trades in a day will net you $500.

- *Accept the fact that as a scalper you're going to take positions overnight on occasion.* Normally, if you put in a sell order at the close, you may not get filled at an adequate price, especially given that the stock trades at low volume. The trick is to be familiar enough with the range the stocks trade in so that you're comfortable holding overnight at the prices you paid.

- *If you lose more than $3/8$ on a scalping trade, refrain from trading that particular stock again.* Search for something that's more stable.

- *Never use day orders since these are automatically canceled at the end of the day.* Instead use good-till-canceled orders. These guarantee you priority in line at the price you specified in the event you must hold the position overnight.

- *Never use all-or-none orders.* Such orders require that your positions be filled in its entirety or not at all. For that reason they limit your chances of getting the order filled at all.

Chapter Eight
Betting It All
Mary Pugh: The Quintessential Contrarian

What would you do if you'd lost millions in a single stock – a stock of a company very few people had even heard of, one that had dropped by 80 percent? True enough, your gains in the stock still totalled well over $1 million. You could sell right now and call yourself a winner. So would you sell? Or would you hold and risk having the price drop further? Is that your final answer?

This was precisely the dilemma that faced Connecticut investor Mary Pugh in May 2000. Pugh trades from her elegant prairie-style home on the Connecticut shoreline, at times using up to four large-screen monitors that keep her focussed on the markets and chat threads on RagingBull.com, where she has been among the most prolific posters. Sometimes trading consumes her so much, she says that she "zones out," just watching the screens, and forgets whether or not she's eaten lunch. "I used to have a housekeeper for 17 years," Pugh says. "She would bring me food. So I would make sure I had breakfast, lunch, and dinner. Now, on my own, what I do is say, 'Oh my God, I've got to eat!' So I run upstairs, I make myself a sandwich and clean it up and come back down. And then 45 minutes later I say, 'Oh my God, I've got to eat,' so I run back upstairs, I make myself another sandwich."

In the course of her trading, she's discovered what it's like to make and lose millions in the market. It's ironic that her own portfolio has experienced so many gut-wrenching ups and downs, because Pugh is one of the most calculating investors you'll meet. Indeed, the way she invests in the market resembles the way a pilot flies a plane. Just like a pilot going over a flight plan, Pugh thoroughly researches the stock's fundamentals before entering a position. When she makes her move, she's as focused as a day trader, watching the market indicators – again, just like a pilot studies the instruments in the cockpit during takeoff. But once Pugh reaches cruising altitude, things tend to pretty much run themselves. In other words, she won't think much about the stock as long as it's on course to the price target she's specified. Think of a plane flying on autopilot. Finally, when it's time to exit the position, Pugh becomes that totally focused day trader once again, watching her stock and the market as a whole as she carefully eases out of her position. This strategy allowed her to pilot a portfolio that grew from virtually nothing to several million dollars before the ahem crash of April 2000. Not bad, considering her at-home trading must fit in between stints as a business consultant.

Fundamentally contrarian

Like a lot of successful investors, Pugh has mixed and matched investment styles over the years and dabbled in different investment venues – everything from blue chips to Internet high flyers to so-called penny stocks. But if there's a common thread that runs through all her investment strategies, it's good old-fashioned contrarianism, the belief that you should do the opposite of what the majority of investors are doing at any given moment. Accordingly, Pugh says she'll listen closely to what her broker tells her, what analysts tell her, and what the fund manager on CNBC has to say that day. And then quite often she'll do what she wants.

Pugh's contrarian approach goes back more than two decades. After receiving an M.B.A. from Columbia University in New York, she went to work as an assistant account executive for ad agency Ogilvy and Mather – a job that made her feel a little like a square peg in a round hole. "Marketing people back in '77, when I first got into the business, tended to be more glad-handing rah-rah types." She says. "But these types fell short on analytical skills." Over the years, she put together marketing programs for familiar companies like American Home Products, Guinness, Nestle, and Johnson and Johnson. As her responsibilities grew, she began managing entire marketing programs – which forced her to do a certain amount of glad-handing of her own. But she says her real strength was in analyzing the entire business from the point of view of its products. How much money could these products realistically be expected to make, and how might that positively effect the company's margins and its bottom line? To find the answers, she created detailed P&L statements whenever she studied a new product – just like a financial analyst.

Quickly she came to realize how her unique skills could also be put to work investing in stocks. "A marketing person is someone who can understand trends and can see things coming down the pike, "she says. "Combine that with someone who's analytical. What better skill set is there for running around and picking stocks?"

The stocks she like best, she discovered, were those that offered hidden value. You could say the first stocks she bought, starting around 1982, were textbook contrarian plays. Prime example: Throughout the Midwest at the time, farms were wallowing in bankruptcy, victims of high interest rates and increased foreign competition. On a hunch, Pugh checked out the *Wall Street Journal*. Sure enough, the stocks of farm equipment suppliers like Caterpillar Inc. (CAT) were selling at deep discounts. And she bought in and rode then up.

> With fraudulent schemes running rampant on the Net, It's no wonder short selling was popular since for short sellers there is as much money to be make riding scam dog stocks back down to the gutter as there is running them up during the pump phase.

During that same period, U.S. automakers were also taking their lumps. "Everyone thought the Japanese would eat Detroit alive," she says. "I studied the American car business, and I said, "I think that the one auto company that is going to change over the fastest was Ford." The Ford stock she bought in 1986 rose by 25 percent – a nice run in that – pre-Internet bull market era. Pugh figured she was on to something.

Everything you know is wrong

Contrarian investing is sometimes confused with value investing – although the difference may be one of degree. Value investors look for bargain stocks, that is, companies whose numbers show they're worth more than the price tags investors have put on them. Value investors used to say that Disney was undervalued, for example, because the real worth of its vault of classic movies is greatly understated on the company's books. Contrarians go a step further, they look for companies or perhaps entire sectors that have lost all respect among investors. They buy when all the signals say sell. And conversely, they sell when all the signals tell them to buy. "Buy panic; sell euphoria" is a popular contrarian motto.

Here's an example of how that strategy can work. Back in 1998-1999, oil was flowing freely and cheaply. OPEC was in total disarray. And stocks of oil drillers and the like resided in the gutter. With oil so cheap, it just didn't pay to search for new reserves. For contrarians, the very fact that everyone was trashing oil stocks was reason enough to consider buying. Analysts touted the sector in *Wall Street Journal* articles and on CNBC. But for months, the stocks remained downtrodden. Oddly enough, the bottom those stocks reached became a time of above-average insider buying. The meaning should have been crystal clear to all investors. Those who understood the industry best – the insiders – knew a bargain when they saw one. That insider buying marked the starting point for energy prices' long march upward.

Even in the face of overwhelming evidence such as insider buying, being a contrarian is no easy task. That's because we're all taught from an early age that the majority is always right. After all a unanimous vote can send someone to the electric chair. Chillingly, perhaps, contrarians will tell you that the very moment everyone starts holding the same opinion, that opinion's about to change. The logic of this way of thinking appears both simple and irrefutable. When everyone who believes in a stock has already bought it, that becomes precisely the point when no additional buyers can be found. Consequently, the stock can't rise any higher. So it will likely fall. The same holds true of markets as a whole, especially when they suffer severe bouts of irrational exuberance. For example, in March – April 2000, as the NASDAQ roared to over 5,000, everyone happily proclaimed that the boom in tech stocks would last forever. People who should have known better, even the most conservative market analysts, began believing that it really didn't matter if a company had earnings. Or who cared if its price/earnings multiple hovered north of 10,000?

To a contrarian, all of this looked like a perfectly scripted disaster scenario. All through the bull market of the late '90s contrarians like Warren Buffet and James O'Shaughnessy were regarded as mad prophets in the wilderness. Or at best annoyances. No one listened. That is, until the market crash. Then everyone listened.

❝ When everyone who believes in a stock has already bought it, that becomes precisely the point when no additional buyers can be found. Consequently, the stock can't rise any higher. So it will likely fall. ❞

Of course, contrarianism is a soft science at best. Calculating, analytical types that they are, contrarians seldom make judgments based solely on their perception of news events. They perform the necessary due diligence. They research both the stock's fundamentals and its technicals. In the case of last spring's market crash, they could have turned to technical analysis to see that the rise in the markets was every-steepening. A dangerous sign since nothing goes straight up forever. Likewise, they could have looked at insider selling and found that it too had risen.

When investing in individual stocks, they have to do a fair amount of fundamental research as well. Some contrarians in addition follow specific rules: Anthony M. Gallea and William Patalon III, in their book *Contrarian Investing*, say you should never buy a stock until it's fallen by at least 50 percent. Then expect a three-year wait before the stock rebound. The largest gains will come in the second and third years.

The two authors also made the point that contrarian stocks tend to be more volatile than your average stock, which would seemingly make them appealing to momentum and growth investors. The contrarian approach, as Gallea and Patalon explain, is to find volatile stocks that have the maximum amount of bad news priced into them. That way, everyone who's liable to sell the stock has already sold it. Therefore, no further selling will drive the price down. Any subsequent volatility will be on the upside.

Powered by Microsoft

As a contrarian, Mary Pugh also learned to back her hunches with painstaking due diligence. Borrowing from her marketing background, she devised her own methods of judging a company's financials in order to predict its future earnings. She'll start poring over its numbers by going to Web sites like Edgar-Online.com, which maintains a database of public companies' official reports to the SEC. These reports include detailed financials – what you see in an annual report or quarterly statement. Pugh will use these figures to devise her own P&L for the company. But hers will attempt to look into the future. If, for example, the company's about to debut a new product, Pugh will try to predict its likely market share. What revenues might the company expect from the product? And how will those revenues affect the company's future margins? Armed with that data, she'll next try to see what investors are currently paying for those same earnings at similar companies – that is, companies within the same sector. "Let's say wireless chipmakers are all selling at price/earnings multiples of 30," Pugh explains. "Then I apply a range of P/Es based on that," she says. That range of P/Es will translate into a series of target prices for the stock. For example, most of the time investors will pay a multiple of 30 for the stock. But some companies in the sector sell at multiples of 25 and some at 40. Her target prices might therefore come in with earnings multiples of 25, 30, and 40. As the stock approaches each of these targets, she'll sell a portion of her holdings. Pugh's method of analysis closely resembles the way institutional investors deconstruct a stock. So why not simply look at an analyst's consensus projections something you can easily find at Web sites like Zacks.com? Because Pugh believes her own method is superior. The reason: Her targets follow how investors track a stock. "It's the investors who determine the price of the stock," she says. "It's not analysts."

Early on, Pugh began building elaborate Excel spreadsheets to plot out her projections. Then around '92 she decided to invest in the company that made the software: Microsoft (MSFT). And that too was a contrarian play of sorts. Apple Computer, still a credible contender to Microsoft in those days, was going after the school market and creative market, she says. "Everybody in my business, that is advertising, was using Apple. But meanwhile my clients were using IBM. And I thought, "Hmmmm, who is there more of, these corporate people or these creative people? And I said, 'There are more corporate people.' That's when I bought my first 100 shares of Microsoft."

The way Pugh built her position in Microsoft was even more contrary. "The first Microsoft Windows product was not that great," she says. "Whenever there was bad news about Microsoft, that a new bug had been discovered in the program, I'd buy." Between '92 and '96, Pugh made a series of small investments – a few thousand at a time – in Microsoft stock as it climbed relentlessly and split numerous times along the way. By the end of 1996 those shares were worth roughly half a million dollars.

Fortunes lost and found

A tidy sum indeed. Unfortunately, fate has a way of screwing things up. Pugh got a divorce. She and her husband split their portfolios. During 1998 a market crash and the choppy conditions that followed reduced her holdings substantially. But significantly she'd placed a large chunk of her portfolio in a Roth IRA. Which meant, of course, that any subsequent gains would come tax-free. "That was the starting point for my serious investing," she says.

"What more fortuitous time for someone to jump into the market?" she says. This was the end of the crash and the start of the outrageous Internet stock bubble. Pugh bought stocks like Yahoo (YHOO), Amazon (AMZN) Network

Solutions (NASC), Checkfree (CKFR), Iomega (IOM), Dell (Dell), and American Online (AOL). And with the exception of Iomega, she says, everything started heading through the roof. By January, Pugh's portfolio made her a paper millionaire.

To celebrate the event, her broker sent her a bottle for champagne. Yes, up until this time she had been using a traditional broker and paying out thousands in commissions, even though she was doing most of the research herself. "In February I decided that I wasn't comfortable holding Amazon and Yahoo. I had maybe 20 different stocks. I wanted to consolidate. So I sold off just about everything, and I focused my money in four stocks: Microsoft, CMGI, AOL, and Excite@Home [ATHM]." Literally, two days later Yahoo and some of the other stocks she had sold began crashing, she recalls. Meanwhile, the stocks she'd heavied up on continued to climb through the spring of '99.

Which didn't exactly make her broker happy. Or maybe he saw the handwriting on the wall, because he warned her about putting too much of her money in technology stocks. Owing to her value as a client, he promised to set up a personal meeting between Pugh and the brokerage's top stock analysts. And he recommended that she tuck away a good chunk of her money in bonds for safekeeping and diversify across sectors.

Pugh followed some of her broker's recommendations. She bought a rock-crushing company and an insurance firm based on his counsel. In hindsight, she figures she missed out on $160,000 in potential gains because of her broker's picks. "So I called up and said we're going to make some changes here, 'Sell the rock crusher!'" At that point, she transferred the bulk of her money to online broker A.B. Watley.

Short stories

To many people the experience of going from a traditional tell-me-what-kind-of-stocks-I-should-buy kind of broker to an online investment account can be a little like going from a small town in North Dakota to Times Square, Manhattan. Suddenly, you're no longer dealing with the market; you are the market. And all the numbers and data that represent the market's vital signs can cause information overload. That's the way Pugh felt the first time she saw A.B. Watley's Level II screen, the kind of detailed stock ticker that day traders use. Instead of one price, the Level II screen showed all the top bids and offers to buy and sell stocks. Moreover, those offers constantly changed before your eyes – and not only the numbers but their colors changed as well, depending on whether the stock was up or down for the day. First time she powered up the Level II screen it looked like something from an air traffic control room and she wanted to run from the room.

In the weeks that followed, she and her son tried to figure out what all the numbers meant. Then, as it happened, all the empowering trading tools made available by her online brokerage account made Pugh – the avowed contrarian – embark on a kind of quest, dabbling in different investment styles. It was a quest that would ultimately lead to an obscure software company and her biggest win yet. However, before that happened, Pugh tried day trading and found she didn't especially like it. When her accounts didn't clear fast enough, she'd receive the dreaded margin calls. Sometime later she attended a seminar from Anthony Elgindy, the infamous short seller.

❝ To many people the experience of going from a traditional tell-me-what-kind-of-stocks-I-should-buy kind of broker to an online investment account can be a little like going from a small town in North Dakota to Times Square, Manhattan. Suddenly, you're no longer dealing with the market; you are the market. ❞

By selling short, of course, you profit when a stock declines in price. And Elgindy believes this is one of the surest ways to beat Wall Street pros at their own game. He operates on the controversial premise that individual investors serve a singular purpose on Wall Street. They exist to sop up liquidity, to hold the bag when stocks dive, to be the fall guy or the mark, depending on what is needed at the time. And at no time has this been more the case than in our current era of Internet IPOs. Indeed, according to Elgindy and others, the brokers, the investment banks, the venture capital companies are all part of a process with one simple objective: to convince the average investor to buy stocks even though they possess ridiculous valuations. And that's the companies that aren't out-and-out pump-and-dump scams to begin with. Once average investors recognize that they are nothing more than brightly illuminated targets used by Wall Street pros, selling short becomes the only sane strategy. Elgindy's views perhaps represent contrarian investing at its most extreme. Yet many traders think enough of his advice on which stocks to short and when that they pay $600 per month to be a part of the chat room he runs called Anthony@Pacific's Research and Discussion Club (www.anthonypacific.com).

Although many beginning investors are confused by short selling, the mechanics of it are pretty simple. Usually your online broker's order entry interface will let you elect to sell a stock short the same way you click on "buy" or "sell" shares. But that belies the fact that important things are happening behind the scenes. Let's say you sell short 100 shares of Qualcomm (QCOM). What's really happening is that your broker in essence, lends you those shares. And you sell them on the open market for the going price. The cash from that sale gets deposited in your account. If all goes according to plan, the Qualcomm shares you sold short will decline in price. At some point, you elect to buy back the shares at their new lower price. This is usually as simple as clicking on the "buy to cover" button on your broker's order entry system. Any difference in price between what you originally sold the shares for and what you bought them back for represents profit. Here's how the numbers might look:

June: Sell short 100 shares of Qualcomm at 66.5	=	$6,650
July: Bought to cover 100 shares of Qualcomm at 55.75	=	$5,575
Profit	=	$1,075

Piece of cake, right? But suppose things don't go as planned? Qualcomm announces better than expected earnings, and the stock soars in price. You lose. And as the stock continues to rise in price, your broker may ask that you add funds to your margin account to ensure that you're able to re-purchase the stock you borrowed at its current higher price. Again, here are the numbers:

June: Sell short 100 shares of Qualcomm at 66.5	=	$6,650
July: Bought to cover 100 shares of Qualcomm at 75.75	=	$7,575
Loss	=	$1,075

Tough break. And it could get worse if Qualcomm went on a tear and continued rising, as tech stocks have been known to do.

Rats die!

Because it's a sound company with a seemingly bright future, a sector leader like Qualcomm can therefore be a dangerous choice for short sellers. But a scam dog stock would constitute the ultimate short play. As described in John R. Emshwiller's book *Scam Dogs and Mo-Mo Mamas*, a "scam dog" stock is one that is overvalued and potentially fraudulent at the same time – an enticing combination for short sellers, since the higher they climb the harder they fall. And being an out-and-out fraud of a company, a scam dog might even fall to zero.

After her seminar with Elgindy, Pugh came to believe that a lot of low-priced, so-called penny stocks were scam dogs. And here again she called upon her background as a marketing analyst to ferret out those companies that were. By going to Edgar-Online.com, she would look for frequent management changes. And like other short sellers, she might study historical charts seeing if the stock rose or fell with heavy volume and in the absence of news.

Pugh was deep into her short-selling phase during the fall of '99, a time when nearly all technology stocks were racing skyward. Scam dog stocks and those pumped up by unsavoury elements were popping up everywhere. In June 2000 the *Wall Street Journal* proclaimed that "the long running bull market has made stock manipulation the white collar crime of choice – even among organized crime figures." June was the month the Justice Department indicted 120 people, some with alleged ties to the nation's five largest organized crime families. It was the biggest one-day securities fraud sweep ever. It resulted from an alleged scam that the feds claimed had milked investors out of $50 million. Mob influence, according to the *Journal* article, appears concentrated in micro-cap stocks, that is small companies with market capitalizations of roughly $250 million or less. Owing to their size, only a few thousand shares of these companies normally trade on any given day which makes these stocks highly illiquid and especially easy to manipulate. This can even occur when the companies' management is clueless as to what's happening. That's what happened with Learners World, a company that runs three Brooklyn, New York, day care centers. The stock normally traded at 25 cents per share. But in the space of just a few days it jumped to nearly $10. And then it nose-dived to 19 cents per share. Learners World's manic roller-coaster ride classically illustrates how pump-and-dump schemes operate, according to the allegations. Learners World, acting in good faith, retained a Florida consultant and underwent a 1-30 reverse stock split. This allowed the number of shares in the total float to be reduced 30-fold. The smaller the float, of course, the easier it becomes to manipulate the stock. In addition to the reverse split, the company also distributed blocks of what are called "restricted common shares" to its own directors. These shares enabled the directors to maintain voting control of the company. However, regulations prevented them from selling their shares on the open market. All the shares that could be traded were controlled by the consultant. And he was therefore allegedly able to manipulate the price through a series of phony transactions between several bogus brokerage accounts. Again according to allegations, these accounts were set up by a man who allegedly had ties with the Columbo organized crime family. Meanwhile, Learners World issued a series of press releases touting the company's planned Internet strategy. As the shares rose, they attracted the attention of individual investors and rose even higher. When those involved in the alleged scam reasoned the shares had peaked, they dumped them. And the stock dive-bombed.

But that was just one example of how mob-backed pump-and-dump scams allegedly operated. According to Justice Department allegations, members of the Bonano and Columbo crime families formed an alliance with the nation's other top crime families and then moved in to control a handful of small brokerage firms. Brokers at these firms were told which stocks to hype to their clients. Those who refused were threatened with beatings.

Of course, the business of stock manipulation could get a lot nastier than that. In October 1999, two traders, Maier Lehmann and Albert Alain Chalem, with close ties to Wall Street were found dead in Chalem's home in a high-end suburban New Jersey neighbourhood. According to *Business Week*, Chalem, a stock promoter born in France, in particular maintained a labyrinthine arrangement of corporations and investment deals throughout the globe, including Israel and Eastern Europe. He had reputed ties to organized crime figures going back several years. The fact that he was shot in the eyes, ears, and mouth indicates his murder was some form of grisly ritual execution – one intended to convey a message. Some mob insiders speculate that he was killed for informing to the feds. As one noted, "Rats die."

But it's investors who are more routinely bludgeoned, at least metaphorically. And that bludgeoning doesn't have to come from the mob. Internet chat rooms are rife with posts aimed at influencing the price of thinly traded stocks. U.S. Attorney Mary Jo White, who indicted two alleged Internet fraudmongers, calls these chat rooms "virtual boiler rooms," after the boiler room operations in which brokers hawk scam dog or nonexistent companies to unsuspecting clients. "This is the dark side of the Internet," she said in a statement following the indictment. "Determined fraudsters can swindle a virtual audience by taking large positions in thinly traded stocks, disseminating hundreds of thousands of spam e-mails touting these stocks and then sell them into the fraudulently inflated market they have created."

A Georgetown University law student perhaps put it more succinctly in a post he allegedly placed on the Web. "Buy a bunch of garbage stock. Tell your idiot subscribers about how great the stock is, and like sheep they will run out and buy it. Dump the shares you bought a few hours ago to all these suckers." In fact, this was exactly what the student is said to have done. His alleged scheme centred on a bogus stock tipsheet he distributed over the Internet to more than 9,000 subscribers. He and his colleagues allegedly received $345,000 from the scam before the SEC filed a complaint against him.

Yun Soo Oh Park (a.k.a. Tokyo Joe) is another trader who came under the SEC's scrutiny. Before he became an Internet stock-picking guru, Park according to some accounts spent time in a Mexican jail and served as a medicine man for a Sri Lankan village. More recently he was in the restaurant business in New York. But Park is best known for his chat room, Tokyo Joe's Societe Anonyme (www.tokyojoe.com), where traders reportedly pay up to $200 a month for his recommendations. The SEC claims that on "numerous occasions" Park hyped stocks to his subscribers and then sold them those same stocks from his own inventory. Allegedly, the fractional gains he made from July 1998 to June 1999 amounted to hundreds of thousands of dollars.

Long shots

With fraudulent schemes seemingly running rampant on the Net, it's no wonder short selling would be popular, since for short sellers there is as much money to be made riding scam dog stocks back down to the gutter as there is running them up during the pump phase. The important difference of course, is that selling scam dogs short is decidedly legal, assuming of course, you don't try to manipulate the price down.

" Investing in penny stocks is perhaps the ultimate contrarian play. These are companies the market has relegated to the proverbial trash heap. Why else would they cost just 9 cents per share? "

However, Pugh in the end rejected the whole idea of short selling. Because she said, it was downright dangerous. "To me it's a bad bet," Pugh says. "And the reason it's a bad bet is the unlimited downside and limited upside." True enough. A stock can't go any lower than zero. But that spread from zero to its current price represents the maximum upside for a short seller. On the other hand, a stock can increase in value thousands of times – something especially true of penny stocks that can rise literally from just pennies a share to $30 or more. That was where Pugh decided to focus her attention – on long shots.

Investing in penny stocks is perhaps the ultimate contrarian play. These are companies the market has relegated to the proverbial trash heap. Why else would they cost just 9 cents per share? In many cases they may have been delisted from the major exchanges for failing to meet their revenue requirements. Instead they are relegated to the less stringent over-the-counter market.

Nevertheless, Pugh reasoned, since Anthony Elgindy had taught her how to detect the frauds from the true gems, why not focus on the gems? Here again, her background in marketing had taught her to research stocks the same way she researched products. She felt confident she could separate the scam dogs from the winners. In addition to poring over the numbers at Edgar-Online.com, she investigated what people had to say about the companies on the penny stock threads of popular investment boards like Raging Bull, Yahoo, and Silicon Investor. It was simply a matter of entering a ticker symbol and then reading what people had to say. Although these threads, like the stocks they discussed, could be rife with scams, Pugh reasoned she could separate the honest and accurate posts from the sleazy ones. Pugh's search for killer low-priced stocks led her to buy a series of small technology firms, among them Merchant Online (MRTO), a Boca Raton, Florida, company that provided turnkey Web hosting for e-commerce companies. She also bought Mitek systems (MITK), a San Diego company that makes character recognition software and American Technology Corp. (ATCO), another San Diego company that develops acoustic software.

Naturally, that parabolic autumn and winter of the market's long bull run saw all technology stocks rise like phoenixes on steroids – only to melt later, of course. But just as another trader Teresa Lo (see page 11) had discovered with gold stocks, it was the third- and fourth-tier penny stocks that showed the greatest percentage gains throughout the market's madcap climb. If investing in penny stocks was the ultimate contrarian play, it also might provide the ultimate payout.

That in fact was exactly what happened with the stock Pugh eventually decided to focus all of her attention on: e.Digital Corporation (EDIG).

Letting it all ride

Like American Technology Corp. and Mitek Systems, e.Digital also hailed from San Diego. However, in comparison to these other two technology companies, e.Digital's potential market appeared huge. The company possessed an operating system compact enough to manage memory in everything from digital camcorders to digital music players, personal digital assistants, and the like – in short, all the devices that will soon interact with one another in the grand wireless web that techies have promised is just over the horizon. The marketer in Pugh loved the idea that these devices might be in everyone's hands within several years. When she worked out her own P&L for the company, it told her the stock would eventually increase by upward of 40-fold. e.Digital's tiny OS could become the Windows of the wireless world. What's more, the feisty contrarian in Pugh loved the idea that shares were trading in the toilet – around 70 cents each when she began accumulating. Also, information on the company was difficult to come by. Clearly e.Digital was a find. And just as she'd done before when selling off her holdings in order to focus on a short list of winning stocks, Pugh took profits in the other penny stocks she owned and put everything down on e.Digital. Her holdings increased to the point where she could count on getting VIP treatment whenever she decided to visit the company. Conversation about e.Digital began to dominate her thread on Raging Bull. And there was even talk that she should request a board seat something she says she has no interest in doing.

Meanwhile, the stock continued to climb. And when e.Digital finally peaked at just under 25 in January 2000, Pugh's entire portfolio, which by this time consisted largely of e.Digital stock, climbed to somewhere around $7 million.

It would be great to report that Pugh, sensing the market top, sold all of her e.Digital at the high, pocketed her profits and moved to St. Bart's. But that would neglect the fact that she is a contrarian. Pugh held on through the crash as EDIG slipped to around $5. Although her holdings were still in the black, her losses on the stock totalled close $6 million (calculated from the stock's brief 52-week high). Yet throughout the tumultuous decline, Pugh insists she had her eyes fixed on the long term. "You have to understand that my target price was not $24. My target price was higher than that." All too often in the past, she says, she'd sold off stock only to see it recover and then rise even higher in the following months. e.Digital was by far the biggest bet of her investing career, and she was determined to see it to the end – like some pilots who realize that the safest course in choppy weather is sticking with the flight plan they so carefully mapped out.

As she'd done with her other stocks, Pugh's flight plan started with the hypothetical P&L statement she constructed for the company. She figures the operating system might license for $8 per copy. That being the case, just a handful of 2-million-unit orders by digital device manufacturers would drive up revenues nicely. And with margins pegged at a conservative 30 percent, the Street would have to take notice, she insists. Similar companies sell at P/Es of 50. Bottom line: Earnings of around $85 million could drive the stock to the mid-$30 range, she believes. That would give e.Digital a market cap of roughly $4.3 billion, and Pugh's own holdings would be worth over $10 million. But Pugh believes the stock has more upside potential as the popularity of wireless devices continues to grow.

When e.Digital reaches a series of target prices she's already devised, she'll carefully sell off chunks of her holdings. "When I do that I will buy back some of my positions that I gave up last fall in Microsoft and AOL," she says, "and I will probably buy some Wal-Mart and CMGI. I love those stocks. I made the money that I put into e.Digital off those stocks. And I don't think they've capped out. When e.Digital hits its next milestone, I'll sell another $2 million worth and just stash it away in bonds or something like that. Then when e.Digital goes to the next milestone, I will sell all but about 25,000 shares. And what I'll do then is figure out what proportion of my money I want to make play. It will probably be around 10 percent. I'll take that 10 percent and begin looking for the next thing that I think is leverageable like an e.Digital. I'll put $300,000 to $500,000 in a company like that."

Mary Pugh's trading rules

- *Don't invest unless you understand the company.* Research it the same way you would if you were creating a marketing plan. Look at the potential markets, forecast the company's ability to capture those markets and compute the revenue. Then use an earnings multiple that's standard for the sector to compute the stock's future price.

- *Buy on bad news.* By doing the fundamental research you can be confident that the long-term prospects for the company are sound. You can then acquire the stock even as other investors drive the price down.

- *Use risk capital to find a variety of companies that could rise in value.* Set target prices for each, and as they reach those target prices sell off your holdings and concentrate them in the company with the greatest long-term growth prospects.

- *Set multiple sell targets for your stock, and sell a percentage of your position when it reaches each target.*

- *Anticipate seasonal market cycles.* The biggest gains are often made in the fall and are followed by a late winter sell-off as people must pay taxes on those gains.

- *Remember that money talks loudest of all.* It's not analysts, it's investors who determine the price of the stock. Therefore, even if a stock has a high or low P/E according to analysts, that P/E is justified because that is what those backing their opinions with their money are saying.

- *Concentrate your holdings in those sectors that you know will be strong long-term moves.* However, if you're going to be in technology, for example, you should diversify yourself across different aspects of the sector. Buy stocks of hardware companies, Internet companies, wireless, and telecommunications companies.

Chapter Nine
Profiting from Good Markets and Bad
Scott Slutsky: Rider of the Storm

The people who hang out at the investment-chat megasite Silicon Investor know Scott Slutsky by his online handle, The Lizard King. The nickname also belonged to Jim Morrison, the deceased lead singer of the rock group "The Doors." But Slutsky's own trading style doesn't seem in any way inspired by the late, manic, and suicidal rock musician. Far from it. Few traders are as methodical and diligent in their approach as Slutsky.

On the other hand, independent-spirited active traders are in some ways this era's version of rock stars. And if that's the case, Slutsky seems to have the trader's lifestyle down to a T. He even has a couple of hundred diehard fans who pay $250 per month to receive stock ideas that he and a partner Jim de Porre (a.k.a. Rev Shark) dispense at a site called Super.traders.Com. Slutsky spends the summer months trading out of his home in a Chicago suburb. The rest of the year he and his wife live in a four-bedroom house built on stilts, located on an isolated and pristine island in Florida. The home sits just half a block from the shimmering waters of Tampa Bay and three blocks from the Gulf. And he can see the bright water from the office where he trades. "It's very mellow down here," he says.

Be nimble, be quick

Slutsky can thank his success at trading for the house. A onetime lawyer from the Chicago area, he eased out of his private practice around 1998 in order to take up trading full-time. Starting with an account of roughly $50,000 he managed to weather the steep market correction in October 1998 and continued to nurture his holdings till they topped seven figures in early 2000. That performance in and of itself isn't all that special within the trading community. A lot of traders watched their accounts mushroom during the heady days from October 1999 to March 2000 – the easy-money times that some believe may never come again. Statistics on traders' earnings are hard to come by. But what is documented is that nearly 200 mutual funds realized triple-digit returns during 1999. And these funds achieved that growth by making conservative buy and sell decisions – at least in comparison to day traders and swing traders.

> **" Slutsky and his wife live in a four-bedroom house built on stilts, located on an isolated and pristine island in Florida. The home sits just half a block from the shimmering waters of Tampa Bay and three blocks from the Gulf. And he can see the bright water from the office where he trades. "**

The point being, if that many funds could double their returns – or better – in just a year, a lot of traders probably made out even better.

The reason for that is simple: Stay-at-home traders have a distinct advantage over fund managers since the former aren't bound by anything like a mutual fund prospectus, a binding legal document that outlines what strategies the fund's managers may use. With no one to answer to save their broker's margin call, trades can go both long and short, as they please, hedge their positions with options, make nail-biting trades on margin, and duck out of positions the instant something goes wrong. "Mutual funds can't do what I can do," says Slutsky. "They can't buy small stocks and get in and out quickly like I can, because they have to buy a big position. And when you're in a thin stock and you want to sell 50,000 shares, you can't get out." Indeed, mutual funds rarely turn over their portfolios as extensively as even the most reticent swing traders. Slutsky, for example, estimates that he made 5,000 trades in 1999.

So if achieving stellar returns during '99 isn't such a big deal, what is it that sets Slutsky apart from his colleagues? The answer, simply put, is that his account climbed to new highs *following* the April 2000 crash. Unlike legendary hedge fund managers such as George Soros and Julian Robertson, who were sorely wounded by the crash, Slutsky and a very few traders like him saw the handwriting on the wall and abandoned ship – without surrendering any of their gains. Equally important, they possessed the skills to trade on the short and perilous bear market rallies that occurred throughout the early spring months of 2000. These traders found their skills amply rewarded during the summer rally that followed.

It's the volume, stupid

What tipped Slutsky off that the bubble was about to burst? Slutsky says he owes his survival to his ability to read charts like a sage. And as he watched the charts during the winter months of 2000, all the indicators pointed to a fall. "The market went parabolic at the beginning of 2000," he says. "A thing that's typical of parabolic markets is that the volume swells like crazy. This volume disguises the fact that there's really a lot of liquidation going on, that a lot of the institutions are getting out." In other words, while the smart money was running for the gates each time the market chalked up another new high, individual investors did just the opposite. The same skyrocketing prices seduced them into jumping in. They served as cannon fodder for the big sellers, sopping up billions in liquidity. These individual investors were joined by momentum traders eager to tag along as Internet stocks like CMGI and Inktomi (INKT) rocketed skyward. "Stocks were moving up 10-20 points per day," Slutsky recalls. And every rise was met by waves of selling. Institutions sold into the tenuous strength of the high-flying tech stocks, and momentum traders bailed at the last possible moment.

During the mini-corrrections that preceded April's big crash, those same high flyers often dropped by 10 and 20 points per day. Which is why Slutsky has vowed to steer clear of the market's most volatile stocks. "I don't buy stocks that are up $20 in a day," he says. Instead as you'll see, when the dreaded correction came, he shifted into more defensive holdings, trimmed back on others, and then sat back and waited for the inevitable fall.

Arguments and counterarguments

Of course, you don't grow a portfolio 20-fold – that's after deducting living expenses and capital gains taxes – without taking some risk. How did Slutsky, a sole-practitioner lawyer create a portfolio he could retire on in just four years? Best to start at the beginning. What's a lawyer he says, if not a quick study, someone who's able to bone up on all the relevant information needed to attack a case – to become an expert, in other words? And indeed, that's how Slutsky approached trading. If you press, you find the reason he turned to trading was that he was getting bored with lawyering. "I'm filing lawsuits all day long. They're all pretty much the same," he says. A colleague was having some success trading. So Slutsky decided to give it a try.

More precisely, he dove headlong into the topic like he was boning up for a Supreme Court appearance. "Once I like something I want to learn everything I can about it. So I started picking up books and reading as much as I could." As a next step, Slutsky began making small trades, a beginner's tactic many experts advise. "I was trying to play it safe. I was not risking a lot of capital." Gradually, he says, trading started taking up larger chunks of his day.

From his studies, it dawned on Slutsky that small cap stocks were among the best ways to play the market short-term. He could buy 500 to 1,000 shares of stock priced from $10 to $30. If it moved several points, he'd make several hundred or even several thousand over a period of days – a classic beginning, swing-trading style.

Call it beginner's luck or a smart guess, but one trade in particular convinced Slutsky that there could be real money in trading full-time. A medical imaging company called Imatron (IMAT) selling for 3 $7/8$ caught his eye. Slutsky bought 1,000 shares mainly because he liked the volume explosion and the stock's chart. Moreover, he felt that the news on the company's new device for detecting clogged arteries would attract attention overnight, causing the stock to open sharply higher. The next day the stock jumped to more than $8 – which gave him a gain of over $4,000.

Slutsky realized he had to find a lot more stocks like Imatron and time his moves carefully. Here, he figured his background as an attorney would come in handy. Both lawyers and traders must be highly analytical to succeed, he reasoned. "When you're involved n a lawsuit you're always trying to look for angles, things that are going to convince a judge or a jury of your position." Using that same analytical reasoning, Slutsky combed through companies' fundamental data, trying to come up with arguments as to why the stock might go up or down.

The David/Goliath debate

From his analysis, Slutsky found that the valuations on small cap stocks were particularly attractive at the time. This was largely because during the period 1997 – 1998 most investors had their sights set on the market's blue-chip behemoths like IBM and Microsoft. Here was a complete reversal of an idea that had been gospel on Wall Street for well over a decade, namely that small caps made the best growth investments.

Back in 1981, Rolf Banz published the doctoral dissertation he wrote while attending the University of Chicago. In his oft-cited study, Banz concluded that small cap stocks had outperformed large caps between 1926 and 1979. More intriguing, his findings revealed that small caps had performed best between 1931 and 1935 and again between 1941 and 1945, two periods during the previous century when markets were fraught with uncertainty, either from deep depression or war, and certainly periods when you wouldn't expect fledgling companies to attract investor attention. In part because of Banz's study, traditional asset allocation theory generally recommends that aggressive investors put a greater share of their portfolio into small caps, gradually limiting their exposure as they approach retirement.

More recent market performance has cast some doubt on these assumptions, however. The Russell 2000 Small Cap Index actually declined in 86 of the 231 months between 1979 and 1998. If you were a buy-and-hold investor during that period you probably would have done better putting your money in midcaps, which declined in 9 percent fewer months during the same timeframe.

During much of the last decade, buy and hold investors would have done slightly better putting their money into a large cap fund. Such funds returned an impressive 19.04 percent annually from 1993 to 1998, versus 18.34 percent for small cap funds during the same period. The small difference in percentage return is more significant when you consider the added risk investors take on when investing in small caps.

Those of course are the aggregate statistics and they greatly underemphasize the technology/Internet bubble that occurred during the late '90s. For traders who were able to find and then enter and exit the stocks of leading technology companies, small cap stocks represented a boon of unprecedented proportions. If you'd bought $20,000 worth of Dell Computer stock back in 1996 when it was still relatively small, you'd be a millionaire today. Astounding gains also occurred within the highly volatile biotech sector. Analysts from the investment bank Hambrecht and Quist looked at the performance of 24 stocks from 1995 to 1999. Despite wrenching ups and downs, the stocks would have gained 749 percent by the end of the millennium. By contrast, the NASDAQ rose 250 percent during the same period. Biotech's top performers did astoundingly better. IDEC Pharmaceuticals (IDPH) and MedImmune (MEDI) surged 3,526 percent and 3,771 percent, respectively. Clearly, the trick with small caps is to pick your stocks wisely and plan your exits well.

Find the right bait for momentum traders

To find his stocks, Slutsky relies on several methods. Among the first thing he does is pore over earnings statements, looking especially for accelerated earnings growth. Accelerated earnings growth is a hard test of a company. Ideally, each quarter the company must show that it has earned greater and greater profits both in monetary and in percentage terms. In practice, quarter-by-quarter performance can vary for many reasons. Because of that, many traders who look at this indicator focus on long-term trends. If earnings aren't ballooning quarter by quarter, they should at least be rising aggressively year by year.

Common sense would lead you to believe that companies with accelerated earnings growth would make excellent candidates for investment. But Slutsky trades on the idea that the indicator itself – not the company's performance per se – acts as a lure for momentum players. That is, other active traders like himself will see the same indicator and jump in. Many financial experts share a similar view, believing that these traders will progressively move in and out, while riding the stock – perhaps buying on dips and selling on short-term highs. Meantime, the stock's gradual rise will attract less experienced investors who will acquire the stock with an eye toward holding it long-term. By purchasing shares and removing them from circulation, these less experienced investors will help to raise the stock's level of support. At some point in this process the stock will attract the attention of some of the more aggressive fund managers, who will see the opportunity for a gain over several months' time. Again, the net effect is that the support level continues to rise and the stock will continue to make higher highs following each short-term reversal. This whole pattern is exaggerated with small caps because the total number of shares actively traded tend to be a small percentage of the total float. The fewer shares that trade, the easier it is to affect supply and demand.

> **The stock's gradual rise will attract less experienced investors who will acquire the stock with an eye toward holding it long-term. By purchasing shares and removing them from circulation, these less experienced investors will help to raise the stock's level of support.**

What about an exit strategy? Normally Slutsky looks for his exit when he surmises that the smart money is on it way out as well. A good indication of this occurs when the stock trades down for the day on heavy volume, but in the absence of news.

Breakout and support

For every stock that Slutsky buys he has literally hundreds that he watches, studying how each behaves. His database of stocks has at time totaled 1,700 companies, easily rivalling the watch lists maintained by some of the larger brokerage houses. Slutsky says his database is one of the chief reasons he's been successful. At the end of each trading day he'll scan through his entire list of stocks, examining their charts to see how they've performed. The job can take several hours. Slutsky claims he's scanned through enough charts, that he's memorized a lot of them. "I have charts in my head," he says.

As he pores over his database, Slutsky continually grooms it. He'll delete companies that exhibit little chance of performing and add new ones that look promising. As a result, the database will shrink and grow, reflecting the market climate as a whole. During the April 2000 crash, the database shrank to about 1,300 companies. During the summer rally that followed, Slutsky found himself gradually building it back up. As a result, all the stocks on his list are potential winners. "I always wind up having a database of stocks that are strong by the way that I work my charts and by what I add or delete," he says.

One of the sector charts that he found that seemed to be working well was the Oil Service Index (OSX),which trades on the Philadelphia Stock Exchange. "You could just see that the index was going up strong as the market was going down," he says. Thus, Slutsky started buying shares in oil drilling and oil field service stocks, such as Ensco International (ESV) and Baker Hughes Inc. (BHI).

Moving averages

What does Slutsky look for specifically in his charts? To him, the most important indicators are a 50- and 200-day moving average. A moving average for a stock is a series of average prices taken for a defined period of time – say 50 or 200 consecutive days. Other averages could be for as little as 15 one-minute periods. Calculating a moving average by hand would take hours. Fortunately Web sites such as Bigcharts (www.bigcharts.com) do it automatically – and for free. Slutsky subscribes to eSignal (www.esignal.com), an $80-per-month service that gives him real-time data and many more options as to how he constructs his charts.

Using services like eSignal, traders can superimpose the line representing the moving average over the line representing the stock's actual price for the same period. The goal is to discover the near-term trend for the stock. For example, if the stock's price crosses below its moving average after having trended upward, analysts view this as a bearish sign. Conversely, if the stock crosses above its moving average line after having drifted downward, many see this as an opportunity to buy. As with accelerated earnings growth, the indicator in and of itself isn't necessarily important. Its true importance lies in the fact that others trade on the same indicator. "There's no question that a lot of people do technical analysis," he says. "And I think this creates buying pressure."

Case in point: During the summer of 2000, Slutsky noticed that once stocks began trading above their 50-day moving average they suddenly took off. (Of course, the reason Slutsky is able to recognize patterns such as a breakout from a 50-day moving average is because of the countless hours he spends with his charts.) The rise, he says, was a clear sign of other traders' confidence that the stock would continue to increase in price. By pouring money into the stock, they create a self-fulfilling prophecy. "It's psychological that when a stock trades above the 50-day moving average, it starts to act better, because people think that it is a healthy stock and it's okay to buy it, " he says. "You wouldn't think that so many people pay attention to it [the 50-day moving average], but I see it in so many charts now." All that new money put into the stock also tends to accelerate the price rise, and the angle of the curve increases. Again, small cap stocks, with a relatively small number of shares trading accelerate this trend further.

Another tactic Slutsky uses to decide when to enter a position is to find stocks that have resumed trading near their support level. A support level is the price a stock will periodically sink to before climbing in price once again. The explanation for this is that many traders believe they missed out on acquiring the stock before it rose to the point where it was perceived as overvalued. When the stock sinks back down to its support level, these same traders see this as a second opportunity to buy. Like other technical indicators, a support level is also a kind of self-fulfilling prophecy. Traders buy the stock at support confident that other traders will do the same.

Slutsky is particularly eager to buy at support when he notes that the stock has declined on low volume or when the stock at the close of the trading day was on an uptrend. In the former case, you could conclude that the dropoff in price was a result of the temporary lack of interest in the stock by traders. In the absence of news about the company, this could occur simply because other sectors are hotter at the moment. A strong close for the stock indicates that a large group of buyers have enough faith in the stock to hold on to their positions overnight. Slutsky also likes to buy stocks that put in new 52-week highs, on strong volume. These stocks tend to move higher after a breakout, as there is no selling pressure, since every person holding the shares has a profit.

Building positions

Slutsky's method for actually entering a position closely mimics the way institutional traders operate. At first he'll buy a small position. Then he will closely follow the stock's progress. If it dips on low volume, he's not apt to be concerned. If it loses ground on heavy volume, he may lighten his position quickly on the first day of trading and continue to lighten during subsequent down days. After 3-5 consecutive days in which the stock falls, he may exit the position entirely. Also, if the stock reverses quickly, he'll sell quickly in order to preserve as much of his capital as he can. According to Slutsky, the key to successful trading is preservation of capital. "You have to cut losses quickly," he says. "You can always re-buy the stock if it starts to act better."

Many trading experts such as William Eng, in his book *Trading Rules: Strategies for Success*, strongly advocate this very approach. As Eng explains it, traders spend a good deal of time analyzing their entry points but not enough time designing exit strategies should the trade prove faulty. "Managing the position" throughout the holding period is the key to making money, Eng writes, as well as the key to not losing it.

" With each of his stocks, Slutsky seeks to build a core position. And again he'll prune it back during price declines and add to it at the first indication of a turnaround. This strategy helps to minimize losses and amplify gains. **"**

By the same token, if a position appears to be going in his direction, Slutsky will gradually increase the size of his holdings by whatever amount seems appropriate at the time. "I'm not very scientific about it," he says. Again, the indicators he'll look for include a strong close. A stock that closed on its high for the day would be especially nice, even more so if the price rise occurred on increasing volume and there was evidence that large blocks of shares were being bought. In all likelihood the stock would gap up, that is trade higher still, at the market open the following day.

With each of his stocks, Slutsky seeks to build a core position. And again he'll prune it back during price declines and add to it at the first indication of a turnaround. This strategy helps to minimize losses and amplify gains. Selling a portion of his position at the start of a decline allows him to buy the stock back late at a lower price, thus increasing the gains for the stock. Similarly, by adding when his stock climbs he maximizes his gain. "The key is to make sure you don't give up your gain," he says. "There's nothing that feels worse than when you have a real profit and it suddenly turns into a loss."

Also, like many fund managers, Slutsky safeguards his portfolio through diversification. No single position totals more than 5 percent of his entire holdings. As a result, Slutsky may hold as many as 70 positions. To monitor them all, he uses alerts that warn him when any stock is poised for a possible move. Slutsky admits that he would be a more efficient trader if he traded only a handful of stocks at a time, which is the more common practice among day traders and swing traders. At the same time he finds that holding more positions in stocks that are acting well has substantially increased his trading gains as they tend to go higher Slutsky finds that 40-50 positions is the happy medium. Positions might amount to $15,000-$25,000 each. At the time I spoke with him, the largest stock he owned was Jack Henry and Associates (JKHY), which totalled $24,000. The company provides data processing services to financial institutions. And its stock, then trading at just over $50, had risen from $20 in just six months.

Data processing services have been around since the '60s. Jack Henry and Associates hardly qualifies as high tech. But the company illustrates another way Slutsky minimizes risk, by making sure his portfolio includes a variety of sectors. He has held restaurant and energy stocks. Some of these positions – energy stocks, for example – are purely defensive and will become his core holdings in the event of a serious downturn. On the other end of the spectrum are technology stocks. "Nothing moves like a technology stock," he says.

The trading life

The upside of being able to enter and exit sectors such as energy, high tech and the like is that Slutsky is able to catch the momentum wherever he finds it, and lighten up on poor-performing sectors while he's at it. The downside of this strategy is that it's hard work. As typified by Slutsky workday: "In Chicago the market opens at 8:30. I get up at about 7. I work till the market closes," he says. At lunch he'll relent and get some food. But he never leaves his screens. In fact, he'll have four computers going at once, and four 21-inch monitors. In Chicago those computers are hardwired to the Internet with a cable modem. And Slutsky subscribes to several dial-up ISPs in case his cable access goes down. In Florida, the setup is essentially the same, except that his Internet connections is a fractional T1. As for brokers, he has a total of seven brokerage accounts divvied up among several online brokers and direct access brokers. But the bulk of his account sits with Brown and Company, which caters to knowledgeable traders and charges trading fees that start at $5.

When the market closes, Slutsky downloads his charts, reviews them till 5. Afterward he may sleep for a couple of hours, eat some dinner. By 7:30 he's back reading reports, piles of financial magazines or again gazing transfixed at his charts. He rarely goes to bed until after midnight.

And then it's up again the next morning. As a new trading day commences, there you'll find him constantly tweaking and pruning his positions. As alerts sound on is computer he trims back on this tech stock, adds a little here, fusses over that energy chart and waits for yet another stock to make a critical move, always jumping from stock to stock. No wonder he makes 5,000 trades per year. "I don't think most people could work the way I work," he says. It really requires hard work. Otherwise, you can't make it."

I don't care as much about making money as I do about not losing money. The one thing that's gotten me where I am is being out of the market at the right times.

But all the work is better than doing something that doesn't let you use your skills. "When I was a lawyer, it was so boring and monotonous to me," he recalls. "Now I wake up in the morning and I never know what's going to happen with the market. Everyday's new. I can't wait to get out of bed to see what's happening."

Scott Slutsky's trading rules

- *Choose small cap stocks over large caps.* They normally have shares outstanding, that is smaller floats, and their daily or weekly moves are greater in percentage terms than moves made by large caps. The exception to this is the large cap high-flyer stocks such as Brocade Communications Systems Inc. (BRCD), Juniper Networks, Inc. (JNPR), and Extreme Networks (EXTR). "These stocks can move 10 percent or more in a day."

- *Hold stocks only when they continue to perform.* "Good stocks are stocks making you money."

- *When planning your exit strategy, focus on support and resistance.* Pay special attention to stocks making higher highs and lower lows. The former may indicate a breakout or a reversal. "Stocks making lower lows are stocks a trader doesn't want to own."

- *Build a watch list of stocks you like.* Create the list by using stocks putting in new highs, that is stocks with high relative strength and stocks with strong earnings.

- *When acquiring a stock, start with a relatively small number of shares to form a "core position."* Add to this amount incrementally if the stock continues to perform well. Alternately, sell off portions of the position if it performs poorly. Likewise, sell off portions when the stock appears to be reversing when it hits a resistance level. Then look to repurchase those shares once the stock drops to its support and reverses once again. Always be ready to exit the entire position quickly if it threatens to seriously erode.

- *Consider lightening up on all nonperforming positions during days when the market is behaving poorly,* beginning with the worst-performing stocks in your portfolio.

- *Be wary of stocks that rise on lower volume.* Be less concerned about a stock that dips on diminished volume.

- *Never hold a position that accounts for more than 5 percent of your total portfolio.*

- *The most important rule of all for a trader is preservation of capital.* Know when to be in and out of the market. "A good time to be out of the market is when the major indices such as the Dow, the S&P and the NASDAQ are under their 50- and 200-day moving average."

Chapter Ten
When the Market Turns Mean, Turn to Your Friends
Dave Gordon: The Trench Rat

It's another wrenching, painful day in the markets – the kind of day that was all too typical in the spring of 2000. Panic selling. The stock pickers on CNBC warn of even darker days ahead. And when the closing bell tolls, Dave Gordon knows it wasn't ringing for him. "We broke 3200 today," he says over the phone from his Long Island home. He thinks the NASDAQ could drop further still, to 2800 even. And if that happens the devastation will be widespread, he says. "The technology sector could be set back two or three years if things really crap out. You've got to believe that if people totally lose confidence and all the margin guys are wiped out, the people that rode this stuff down and didn't take profits are dead in the water."

Just maybe, I tell him, there are enough people out there waiting on the sidelines to turn things around once we reach a bottom. Gordon, who built a $50,000 portfolio to $1.5 million riding the tech boom on its way up, and who now advises several hundred subscribers at his subscription chat site Trenchrat.com, doesn't think so. "All this cash is just going to sit in money markets making 7 percent. Why should they risk it? If they show 5, 6, 7 percent they'll do better than the market. So they'll just sit. It's like 1994. It's a distinct possibility."

At the time we spoke, Gordon figured his portfolio had endured some fairly substantial losses, thanks to the crash. Like other traders who suddenly found themselves enmeshed in a decidedly unfriendly market, he's been forced to change his tactics quickly. Instead of focusing on longer-term trades of a week to several months, he began watching the market tick by tick. "There's really nothing to trade unless you hang on that machine like a hawk," he says. By *machine*, of course, Gordon means his PC, which displays streaming real-time quotes. "You've got to take singles. You can't even look for doubles or triples – just base hits through the hole and get out."

Strange visions

When you get to know Gordon a little better, you sense that if anyone can ride out this market maelstrom, it's him. Because Gordon's life has been one of beating the odds and then coming back better than before. Flashback to 1996: Gordon is in an entirely different line of work installing and maintaining swimming pools for the wealthy in Long Island, while raising his then-11-year-old son. Out of nowhere, something far worse than a market crash occurred. Doctors diagnosed Gordon with non-Hodgkin's lymphoma, the same type of cancer that killed Jackie Onassis. The doctors gave him six months to live.

> **There's really nothing to trade unless you hang on that machine like a hawk...You've got to take singles. You can't even look for doubles or triples – just base hits through the hole and get out.**

Of course, chemotherapy offered a slim hope. But Gordon was adamant. He didn't want treatment. I saw my mother die of cancer," he says. "I didn't want to go through it. I just wanted to pull a blanket over my head." Then, says Gordon, his sister came up from Florida. "She said, 'You can't do this; you have a son.' She dragged my ass out of here and took me to the doctor and made me go through treatment," says Gordon.

In all, he underwent three courses of chemotherapy. The hard-core routine forced him to give up his swimming pool business. And eventually he found himself flat on is back. "I was in terrible pain," he remembers. "They were giving me tons of morphine. At one point it looked like I was going to die. They gave me injectable morphine to take home. When they give you that stuff to take home, they don't think you're going to make it."

And then, right about when he was at his lowest point, a very odd thing happened. "When I was in the hospital," Gordon remembers "I was on a ton of painkillers. I had a vision of a rat coming up out of a trench. Somehow in my mind I said, 'Rats survive.' You can't kill a rat. You can poison them, shoot them. You can't kill them. So the rat became like a totem. It was a vision and

I held onto it. He was my friend and I took his name." To Gordon, the rat vision proved he could beat his cancer.

But recovery was still a long way off. And meanwhile, Gordon's problems weren't confined to his health. "I had some stocks, and naturally it was all margined. I didn't think I was going to make it out of the hospital so I didn't call my broker, and I didn't check on anything." What happened wasn't pretty. The stocks fell in price while Gordon was bed ridden. Gordon's broker liquidated his margined positions. "So I come out of the hospital," he says. "Not only do I not own any stocks any more, but I owed by broker money. So I said, 'How am I going to do this?'"

That was when Gordon resolved he'd get serious about trading. And in fact that resolution was helped along by another unlikely vision of sorts, he says. "One day I was watching CNBC in the morning and I caught James Cramer," the outspoken former hedge fund manager and co-founder of the financial Web site, The Street.com. Cramer built his reputation in part by championing individual investors. In his daily commentary on TheStreet.com, he shares the plots, rumors, and news from Wall Street's inner sanctums. "First time I ever saw him," says Gordon. "It was infectious. I got on the computer that night, and I e-mailed him, and he answered me." The two struck up a kind of online friendship. "I never asked him about a stock. I asked him about approaches. What to do. And I guess he liked my style, and he singled me out a bit. He gave me a little attention. And it was inspirational.

So maybe trading offered a way for Gordon to get out of debt. Still he admits, "I was scared to death." But there weren't many alternatives. "When you're lying on your back, there's not too many ways to make money. So it was like a trade I had to learn, like an electrician or a plumber." Gordon taught himself how to research stocks using the Net. He also managed to scrape together enough cash to get himself a stake. "What I started with, no one would believe: maybe 50 grand. That was all I had. I cashed in some bonds. And I had a little money in an IRA sitting in Cisco. That was it."

❝ When you're lying on your back, there's not too many ways to make money. So it was like a trade I had to learn, like an electrician or a plumber. ❞

Over time, Gordon says, he made enough through his investments to get out of debt. From there on, he says, the money just grew. Also, he was making friends through his trading, mainly from hanging out in the chat rooms on the financial Web site the Motley Fool (www.fool.com). One of the two brothers who founded the site, Dave Gardner, invited Gordon to start his own message board. And it was this message board that enabled Gordon to build a following. "I gave out a lot of stocks, and they went up, and people started to follow me."

As the bull market raged, Gordon had plenty of competition. There were hundreds if not thousands of what *Online Investor* magazine calls "board lords," people who head up financial discussion threads. Gordon's stock picks made his followers money. But he managed to stand out for another reason. Call it his plain-spokenness, his colorful use of language.

"I had a style," Gordon reflects. "People liked this style." The logical step from leading discussions on the Fool was to create a Web site of his own. And the name for the Web site was an easy choice. It harked back to the rat in Gordon's vision that had crawled out of a trench and helped him beat his cancer. Gordon hired an artist to draw the rat logo. It took the artist two months to come up with a design Gordon liked. The end result looks something like an unofficial Army insignia from the Vietnam era. A friend of Gordon's who'd helped him as an electrician when he was in the pool business signed on to build the Web site. "Little by little, people followed me from the Fool and the Raging Bull," he says.

Shelter from the storm

In many respects Trenchrat.com is similar to the myriad other online financial chat sites that can charge visitors anywhere from $10 to $600 or more per month. (Trenchrat.com charges $25 per month.) Members wax on about stocks they're watching. The chat room's leader usually alerts subscribers to the trades he or she is making. The rooms provide people with an escape from the isolation that comes from trading alone at home. And not surprisingly, each site tends to develop a unique personality. Some are formal and businesslike. At the other extreme there are rooms where flaming e-mails border on verbal abuse. For its part, Trenchrat.com functions as kind of a shelter in a storm, a place where people look out for each other. "In the room we network," says Gordon. "Everybody's got different sources. Plus, there are other brokers in the room who are also talking to other people."

Take a look at the testimonials on the site and you see that Gordon's subscribers seem quite fond of and even protective of him. A few days before his birthday, for example, online well-wishes poured in from subscribers. "I'm the clown, the ringmaster," says Gordon. "I'm the rat. They love when I come on and chat."

While subscribers exchange notes on the market, Gordon's apt to pop in unannounced. "I go in and out," he says. "I go in the morning. I talk to the 20 or 30 people who are there and tell them what I plan to do during that day, if anything. And then I'll go back in a few hours later maybe for half an hour."

"When the market was going up," he recalls, "every night was a party. People would enter the name of a stock with 800 exclamation points after it. The euphoria was incredible, and it lasted for months. Everybody was making money hand over fist. Buying stocks for $5 that would go to $20.

But of course, good times like that can never last. During the more sobering times, especially when the market's having a stormy day, Gordon might send out a consoling e-mail to his subscribers. Some are practically homilies.

> The CSCO foot finally dropped on our necks this morning. Nothing like having another hobnailed boot pressing down on the sector about now! There is no relief in sight here. The only hope to get a better price to sell now is for a violent bear market short covering rally. What to do? As rat has said before: When folks are out in the driveway heaving over the bumper of their cars and swearing they will never own a stock again it will be over. The technical damage is horrendous. It will take time to fill the rest of the gaps. And it will take a lot longer to form a reliable base. There is no rush to buy any of these falling spears. The "already" broken will rebound first after tax-loss selling is out of the way. The newly broken is not yet finished breaking. The money is running from tech. It will eventually return. Rat is sticking to his long-held plan of waiting in the lowest of the low gaps. Trust the charts. Turn down the noise. Remember these lessons we all learned together. There will be another day.

On the surface, this might seem like a Hallmark sympathy card for day traders. But read between the lines, and you realize there's some prescient advice to be had. And at the end of the day, stock-picking advice is the reason Gordon's subscribers ante up their $25 each month. Gordon says his ability to call the market comes naturally. "Ever since I was a little kid I was a great handicapper," he says. "People used to follow me to the window to see what I was betting. I had huge hits at the track, like $20,000, $8,000, $12,000. I once hit a pick 4 for $13,000." And the reason he was able to pick winning horses? Gordon says that came from "an ability to zone in on the program," that is, the racing form. "I'd live with the form," he says. "I'd walk around with it in my back pocket. I'd read it at breakfast, I'd read it at lunch. I'd read it at dinner. When I went to the track, I already knew what I'd be betting. It's like when you buy a stock, you know what you want to buy, you just don't know where to buy it."

Contrary to what you might think, "it's easier to pick stocks than horses," Gordon says. With stocks, "you don't have the human element. You don't have a horse that throws her shoe or steps in a hole. There are too many variables in horse racing."

By contrast, the process of analysis with stocks is far more straightforward. Instead of the racing form, you have charts that track a stock's historical performance. But, Gordon says, before he even focuses on the charts, he pores over the fundamentals. "Once you find a stock fundamentally, then the chart takes over."

To find his stocks, Gordon combs the Web manually. "A lot of the companies I was buying came from news stories and PR releases." For example, he says, suppose "you own a chip stock and then a news release mentions another chip stock. And you run over and find that chip stock. I used to own Cisco," he says. "And I saw ELON [Echelon Corp.] in a news story about Cisco."

Echelon is precisely the kind of company Gordon likes. Its software products enable small devices – everything from service station gasoline pumps to washing machines – to communicate over the Internet. It's a picks-and-shovels play. "When I was a swimming pool salesman I knew that the companies that were making money on pools weren't the installers, but the guys who sold the chlorine and other supplies," Gordon says.

Once Gordon finds a company he likes, he puts it on his watch list, which numbers about 100. Most of those companies tend to be small caps to mid caps, with valuations under $3 billion. Next, he eagerly pores over each company's charts, as if they were racing forms. "Let's say the market is trending up. Stock is trending up. It looks like it might go exponential where the 13-day moving average starts to go up on a sharp angle. And it starts pulling away from the 50-day. I catch it in the 13-day moving average. If the chart is a little weaker, I'll wait on the 50-day moving average. If the chart is weaker than that, I won't touch it."

Why a 13-day moving average, which represents something like 2 $\frac{3}{5}$ weeks of trading time? "Thirteen is very good in an uptrending market," says Gordon, "because the buyers come in quicker. In a downtrending market use a 50- or 200-day. But when a chart's moving up, the supports are usually at the 13-day. That's where you want your buys."

Gordon also looks for specific things before he exits a position. The most obvious one: the short squeeze. Short squeezes occur when traders who short positions in the stock all run for the exits at once, trying to buy back their borrowed shares. As a result, the price tends to spike up radically. "You have two days of insanity," says Gordon. "Where a stock is heavily shorted, news comes out, the stock explodes. The shorts have to keep covering. The stock could run from $90 to $150 in three days. Then you know there's a short squeeze and you'd better get the hell out." The spike in the stock price evaporates just as quickly. And Gordon concedes that he's missed some opportunities. "Usually if I hang around too long. I'll wait till she breaks support and then I'll get out."

With markets turning increasingly nasty, Gordon has turned to another tactic for his bread-and-butter trades – namely gap trading. Stocks gap up or down when they open at a price that's significantly different than where they closed the previous day. Gaps can happen for a variety of reasons. A company might announce unexpectedly good or bad earnings overnight, for example. This usually results in a wide gap. Smaller gaps may occur because the NASDAQ market makers or NYSE specialists have too many or too few shares. This may give

> **❝ Where a stock is heavily shorted, news comes out, the stock explodes. The shorts have to keep covering. The stock could run from $90 to $150 in three days. Then you know there's a short squeeze and you'd better get the hell out. ❞**

them an incentive to drive the price up or down – whatever it takes to correct that imbalance. When that happens the stock could momentarily trade at an artificial price. Then market forces quickly enter in and move the stock to its correct trading level. The gap closes in other words.

"Not all gaps close," says Gordon. "But I'll say 90 percent of then do." The smart play is to either sell into the gap, trading in tandem with the market makers and specialists, or if you're braver, short the gap and cover later.

"They can burn money"

It's not illegal for market makers and specialists to affect the price of the stocks they trade, so long as they do it in the course of maintaining an orderly market – which is their mandate. At times it's a fine line, however. And gapping stocks do routinely sucker in less experienced traders who buy at the open only to watch their positions deteriorate within minutes. One of the functions of Trenchrat.com is to alert traders to these and other tactics perpetrated by the market's heavyweights. Talking to Gordon, you get the idea that indeed it's a nasty world out there.

Here's just one scary scenario: "The hedge funds could bury you," he says. "They have millions of dollars. They have clout. They can run the futures up." By that Gordon means hedge fund managers might buy futures contracts, particularly in the pre-market hours, when volume's especially thin. This acts to drive the price up. "Let's say they buy futures by throwing $50,000 away," says Gordon. "Which makes the futures go up." People believe the market's going to open on a pop. At that point "they [the hedge funds] dump $5 million worth of stock into you. So they burned $50,000 worth of stock to make the futures go up." And in the process made who knows how many millions from selling the stock.

Alternatively, says Gordon, hedge funds may "manipulate the futures down, and people get scared out and then the hedge funds turn and they rally it. You can't compete with these people because they've got deep pockets. They can burn money."

And it's not just the hedge funds. "There's tremendous manipulation going on," says Gordon. "You get whole groups of guys sitting in rooms, just setting up their bids in line and then pulling them all at once. It's easy to do. You find a lightly traded stock and then you scare the crap out of everybody. Everybody's lined up to sell at 12. You're there at 11½ on the bid, your friend's at 11¼, your other friend's at 11⅛. You have six guys. And then all of a sudden you cancel all the bids. What does it look like? It looks like the bottom fell out. So everybody on the other side has sell-at-market orders in. And you're selling at like $2 down."

> **You get whole groups of guys sitting in rooms, just setting up their bids in line and then pulling them all at once. It's easy to do.**

"If you know how the game works and you understand it, at least you have a chance. It's like you're a batter and you can only hit the fastball. What good is that? You've got to hit the curves, too. Otherwise you can't make it."

So what's a little guy to do? "The only way to play this game safe is to buy the best stocks at the right place and then go with the trend," says Gordon. "The way to protect yourself is to know what you're buying – become a fundamentalist. If you're buying JDS Uniphase Corp. (JDSU) and you know that stock is 170, and they screw you for 3 points in the morning, you don't sell into that. Because you know you're holding good stuff."

Of course it always helps to have friends watching out for one another, too.

" So everybody on the other side has sell-at-market orders in. And you're selling at like $2 down. If you know how the game works and you understand it, at least you have a chance. It's like you're a batter and you can only hit the fastball. What good is that? You've got to hit the curves, too. Otherwise you can't make it. **"**

Dave Gordon's trading rules

- *Buy in bulk.* If you hold a large position of several hundred shares, you can trim it back to ease a loss if the stock falls. Holding smaller positions might force you to sell your shares.

- *Use a 13-day moving average.* The 13-day period works best in uptrending markets, since it 's a good measure of buyers rushing to enter the stock.

- *In a downtrending market use a 50- or 200-day moving average for an indication of support levels.*

- *Buy good companies on bad news.* Know that they're good by studying their fundamentals.

- *Stay away from widely held broken companies.* Any rallies in the stock will be short-lived, since large blocks of long-term share holders will want to sell in order to lock in any gains.

- *Invest in pick-and-shovel suppliers, that is, the companies that supply the resources necessary to help front-line companies in short sectors succeed.* The people who make the most money in a gold rush are the vendors who sell miners their picks and shovels.

- *In a choppy market, exit positions whenever you make a short-term gain.*

- *Your entry point is more important than your exit point.* "If you buy it right, you can sell it at a lot of places and make money. If you buy it wrong, you can get stuck."

Chapter Eleven
Secrets of a Techno-Fundamentalist
Barbara Simon: The Earnings Player

Earnings are the magic elixir on which our economy runs. Take away earnings and very quickly the entire capitalist system would roll over and die. Because without the prospect of earnings as a reward, there would be no incentive for entrepreneurs to take risks and build companies. Likewise, there would be no incentive for investors to buy stocks in those companies. Many economists and market analysts will tell you that you can thank earnings for the much-touted "wealth effect" brought on by the '90s bull market. Whether those earnings came about because of low interest rates or because of heightened productivity in the end hardly matters. What does matter is that companies made unprecedented profits during the period. Those profits continued to increase, and so did the price of stocks in those companies.

One of the reasons the market has become so volatile today is that stock prices have built into them the expectation that the company's earnings will continue to rise in a spectacular manner. This expectation has turned quarterly earnings seasons into major media events – as companies publicly confess how much they've made or lost during the previous three months. A negative earnings surprise by a bellwether company such as Yahoo (YHOO) or Cisco (CSCO) can drop the market by 5 percent in a single day, just as a positive earnings surprise by another company can propel the market skywards.

Okay, maybe the above does sound a little overly dramatic. But think how many times you've heard stock pundits on TV proclaim over and over, "It's an earnings-driven market: it's an earnings-driven market"? And even if these analysts are only partially right, Barbara Simon's investment strategy based on earnings would seem to cut to the very core of what moves the market.

Simon sees earnings in their broadest possible context. She believes earnings control the environment a stock trades in before, during, and after a company makes its numbers public. Accordingly, Simon might, for example, buy a stock and sell it in the days before the earnings announcement – essentially buying on the rumor and selling it *before* the news. Alternately, she might short a stock immediately following the company's earnings announcement.

> **❝** A negative earnings surprise by a bellwether company such as Yahoo (YHOO) or Cisco (CSCO) can drop the market by 5 percent in a single day, just as a positive earnings surprise by another company can propel the market skywards. **❞**

Using this strategy, she's built her trading account to more than seven figures in just a few short years. Not bad for someone whose previous job back in the mid-'90s had nothing to do with finance.

The chameleon approach

You might think of graphic design as a dream job for a stay-at-home mom. But Simon didn't like all the deadline stress. The work – largely from her Boca Raton, Florida-area hotel clients – came in feast-or-famine spurts. She'd be going over a project with a client, she says, and "I'd get this prickly feeling. How am I going to do that? I'll have to be up all night!"

One good thing about graphic design: it got Simon on the Internet, downloading stock photography, transmitting completed projects via e-mail. "Because I was doing so much graphic art on the Internet I discovered that – hey – Yahoo has this great financial site." As she visited more and more financial sites, Simon took a second look at her own portfolio, which was limping along with 10 percent annual gains.

"I just decided to sell some of those old companies that were not going anywhere – Con Edison (ED), Brunswick Corp. (BC) – and buy technology companies, which seemed better from [what I learned by] going on the Internet."

Out with haggard old-economy stocks, and in with the new. *Voila!* A strategy was born. "You make a lot more money when you change sectors and you're chameleon-like," she says. "I was in the Internet sector when it was doing great. When the Internet stocks started going down I sold everything and went into pharmaceuticals." At times she's also been in the retail sector. And she's dabbled in insurance, energy, and international stocks.

Yet, whatever sector she might be in, Simon focuses tightly on the company's earnings history. She started out sharing her advice on a Silicon Investor thread where she used the handle "Jenna". Over the years she became that site's most prolific poster. Then in 1999, like a lot of successful traders, she launched her own chat room Market Gems (www.pristine.com/gems.htm). Subscribers pay from $69 per month for advice on when and how to buy stocks poised to rise on the expectations of a good earnings report, and just as critically, when to sell them.

Money makes money

Simon calls the stocks she recommends "earnings plays." The process of finding them starts by rigorously screening more than 8,000 stocks. Stock screens are like search engines that let you find companies that meet your investment criteria. Simon's a heavy user of a subscription stock screening service call Telescan (www.telescan.com), which can search for stocks using numerous technical and fundamental indicators. However, many less robust but free services can be found on the Web, including Yahoo Finance (finance.yahoo.com), CNBC (www.cnbc.com), and Quicken.com (www.quicken.com). With any of these sites' stock screens, you simply enter the parameters you feel are most important. For example, what level of price/earnings ratio are you comfortable with? What's the share price range of the stocks you like? How much volume should a stock trade on each day for you to feel that it's liquid enough? A stock screen might present you with 20-40 questions like these. When you're done answering them all, the screening application which is actually a data-mining tool, pours through reams of financial data to find stocks that match your criteria.

For Simon, one of the most important screening criteria is accelerated earnings. Just like Scott Slutsky (see page 109), she looks for companies that have rising earnings quarter by quarter. And she looks for that pattern to continue, based on analysts' estimates of the company's future earnings performance. Simon especially likes companies with triple-digit or at least high double-digit earnings growth. And she wants daily volume of around 100,000 shares to ensure liquidity.

Simon also pays close attention to something called a PEG ratio. To compute a stock's PEG ratio, take its price/earnings ratio and divide it by its year-over-year growth rate in earnings. (Again, some stock screens allow you to locate stocks based on PEG ratios you specify.) A stock lands on Simon's radar screen when its PEG ratio stands at 2 or 3. "A lot of stocks are still under 1 and doing fine," she says. Among those she's found in the past that fell into the latter category: semiconductor test equipment maker LTX Corp. (LTXX), computer seller Insight Enterprises (NSIT), and e-business service provider IMRGlobal Corp. (IMRS). Simon likes these "little tech stocks that are not high profile, and have normal multiples and normal PEG ratios." Such stocks traditionally trade at a discount compared to the sector as a whole – which is another factor Simon looks for.

Simon's simple yet rigorous screen narrows her selection from 8,000 stocks to a mere 50. These stocks ride on her watch list, which gives her the chance to scrutinize them more closely. The goal, of course, is to find stocks that are poised to make a big move around the time the companies announce earnings.

Tight triggers

The best earnings plays often occur when a company first crosses the threshold of profitability: a relative rarity and hardly a sure thing. To find candidates, Simon looks at analysts' future estimates. Another excellent earnings play would be a stock that receives an analyst upgrade in the days or weeks prior to its earnings announcement. "If you get your stock upgraded a week or two before the earnings report, that is a plus," she says. "You don't usually get that. Maybe 10 to 15 percent of stocks get upgraded before earnings."

Barring an upgrade, Simon will look for stocks to move by small amounts ahead of their earnings announcement. This is a good indication that interest among investors is already building. "The anticipation of a good report will be enough to give you a good trade for that day," she says.

Before Simon actually begins trading a stock she'll try to deduce the potential that such a movement will occur. And she'll set price targets – or "triggers" as she calls them – for each of her target stocks. The triggers might be based on how the stock has traded in past earnings seasons. They function as buy signals that fire when the stock makes its initial move. In some cases, that move might be as little as a fraction of a point.

"My triggers change based on market climate," she says. "My old triggers were very tight." However, as market volatility increases, she's been forced to loosen her triggers a bit - which of course makes trading more difficult and riskier.

"The strongest stocks up until the crash traded in a very tight range," she says. "The range rarely deviated more than 10 or 15 percent off highs. The minute it went below its support level, it would trigger a buy. And the minute it went above the top line of resistance and it spiked up, I would watch for a reversal down and call it a sell. It was very easy, because it was a very simple chart, like a staircase, where the stocks were just going up."

Lessons from 1997 and 2000

Like another trader profiled in this book, Teresa Lo (see page 15), Simon didn't develop her well-crafted strategy overnight. And she suffered the same costly hits from bad trades that newcomers typically experience. In 1997, for example, with the market steadily climbing, Simon grew more and more bold, putting 50 percent of her money into long call options – usually call options on technology stocks – on any given day. On October 28 she saw 25 of her option contracts melt into nothingness. At the end of that day she found herself $35,000 poorer. "I did not have good risk tolerance," she admits now. "I did not check to see how much I could lose."

What helped save her from going back to graphic design were her online trading colleagues. They consoled each other via e-mail. And Simon vowed at the time that she wouldn't hold more than five option positions at a time, and she usually didn't hold them any longer than seven days. In retrospect, the loss was just a momentary blip. Over the course of months, Simon's earnings plays continued to prove rewarding. Her strategy was sound, she believed. On any given day she put $70,000 to $80,000 in the market. And for all her bad experiences, she still chalked up plenty of days that saw gains of $17,000 or more. In a generally up market, she was seeing gains of 65 percent or more per year, betting on a mixture of technology stocks and household-name retailers like Home Depot (HD), Abercrombie and Fitch (ANF), and Ann Taylor (ANN).

Fast forward to the crash of April 2000. Suddenly the rules changed. And Simon had to call upon what she describes as her chameleon-like abilities in order to adapt. "I've been doing earnings plays for four years," she says. "I'm really good at it. But this was the first time I had to change my strategy."

Simon found that instead of selling a stock just prior to its earnings report, she occasionally had better luck shorting the stock either at or before the time companies actually made their earnings announcement. The market's volatility also forced her to widen the range she allowed stocks to trade within before entering or exiting a position. This was a time – you remember – when daily moves of 200 points or more were common. If she set tight triggers – as she'd done in the past – she would get stopped out of a position that might reverse itself shortly thereafter. The increased volatility made it important that she delicately finesse each trade.

When in doubt, move in closer

As the ugly downslides and treacherous bear market rallies continued, Simon quickly realized that it was impossible to predict the market's direction over a period of days. Therefore, she reverted to a strategy many of her trading colleagues had been forced to follow. She focused in on intraday moves, which were more predictable. And she stood ready to exit her positions at an instant's notice. In other words, she became a kind of day trader, riding the market's intraday momentum wherever she could find it.

> Blimps – that is, scarily over-valued stocks – are day trades, says Simon, owing to their volatility. "I would not even consider keeping blimps as long-term holds. But, ironically, these are the stocks that other people like."

As a day trader, Simon first changed the type of chart she was accustomed to looking at. Instead of daily charts, she used 10- or 15-minute charts and tried to identify short-term break-outs, she says. At the same time, she honed her watch list, focusing on stocks that provided the right amount of intraday volatility. "I choose stocks that have 5-point intraday ranges. A $\frac{1}{2}$- or $\frac{1}{4}$-point move: I don't even look at that. If I'm not making 4 points in a day on shorts or longs, then I don't have a great trade. My trades are planned on 2 or 3 hours. Unless I'm losing. I'm not planning to hold for 15 minutes."

As a day trader, Simon also became religious about going flat at the market close, meaning she often exited all her day trading positions and let the money sit in cash overnight. However, she says, certain circumstances would prompt her to hold a stock overnight. "I would not hold a stock overnight unless the broad indicators were supporting any upward move in the market" the following day, she says. "Otherwise the stock gets caught up in the market downshift." Another reason to hold a position overnight might be when a stock has bucked the trend during the previous day's trading. "If the stock is trading way above its down levels and earnings reports are coming," she says, "and it has bucked the trend in the morning, then I would hold it till the next day.

Unless the market was down 240 points. So market indicators are very important, but mostly to determine whether or not to hold overnight."

❝As the ugly downslides and treacherous bear market rallies continued, Simon quickly realized that it was impossible to predict the market's direction over a period of days. Therefore, she...focused in on intraday moves...and she stood ready to exit her positions at an instant's notice. ❞

Throughout this time, Simon also devised rules on how much of her portfolio she'd allocate to day trading. She uses a six-figure trading portfolio, 40 percent of which is applied to day trading and swing trading. "To me long-term is 4 months," she says. Long-term holdings amount to 12-13 percent of her portfolio. The rest is in more conservative investments. When day trading or swing trading she prefers to concentrate her holdings in a few large positions of 1,000 to 2,000 shares. That way, a 4-point move would give her $4,000 to $8,000 for the day.

Options versus selling short

Some of Simon's day trades and swing trades make use of options as a way to gain leverage while minimizing risk. (For a brief explanation of how options work, see page 16). For example, Simon has used put options because she considers them a powerful substitute for short selling a stock. For example, suppose a company announced disappointing earnings. Traders mercilessly bid down the stock's price, which continues to fall over the course of that day and perhaps the next. If the volume was unusually heavy and the stock's downward momentum was especially strong, short sellers would have a difficult time entering a position. That's because NASDAQ and NYSE regulations prohibit you from selling a stock short unless it price up-ticks; that is, unless the stock's price moves up fractionally from its most recent sale. For that reason, if the stock moves down relentlessly, finding an entry point to short it can be nigh impossible. Remember, your sell-short order is competing with similar orders from hundreds, perhaps thousands of other traders.

Here's how buying puts serves as an alternative. First, you can enter the position at any time and without worrying about the up-tick rule. Also, because any put you buy gives you the right to *sell* the shares at a designated strike price, puts *increase* in value as the price of the underlying stock declines. Therefore you can resell the put you bought at a profit.

Simon has opted for puts that are "deep in the money" – which is the technical term for puts that possess a strike price considerably higher than the current price of the stock. There are several important reasons that traders like Simon use deep-in-the-money puts: For one thing, deep-in-the-money puts offer some leeway in case the stock rallies – namely their value is less likely to completely evaporate. Also, buying deep-in-the-money puts will tie up less cash than shorting actual shares. And because the puts are deep in the money, just like the actual stock they will in all probability retain a certain amount of their value up until their expiration day, even if the stock rebounds before the puts are sold. But most important, deep-in-the-money puts will increase in value more or less in tandem with any downward price move of the underlying stock. In other words, for every dollar the underlying stock declines, the put will very likely gain a dollar.

In addition to buying puts, Simon will occasionally buy call options in advance of an earnings announcement – but only if she's exceptionally bullish on the stock. As was the case with puts, she often prefers calls that are in the money. Remember that by purchasing a call you acquire the right to buy a stock at the call's strike price. Therefore, in-the-money calls have strike prices below the current price of the underlying stock. Again, as with in-the-money puts, calls that are in the money will rise and fall roughly in tandem with the under-lying stock.

"Options for me are just leverage for expensive stock," she says. "And stocks that are moving in fast markets. So I can spend $6,000 instead of $80,000."

That added leverage can also minimize risk. If you pay $6 ($600 per contract) for an in-the-money option on XYZ stock selling for $40 per share, $6 represents the maximum amount you can lose should the company declare disappointing earnings. By contrast, XYZ stock itself might tumble $10, $12, or more on the bad news. So if you owned the shares, you could be out $1,000 or more. On the other hand, because the call is in the money, it will follow the stock price up roughly dollar for dollar. So if XYZ stunned the Street with blowout earnings, and its stock soared to $50, the call could increase from $10 to $16 in the short term. You'd make the same amount of money as if you'd owned the actual shares, but you'd tie up a lot less of your capital in the process.

As with other aspects of her trading, Simon has devised precise rules governing her options trading. She doesn't like to hold long options for more than three days. And she'll typically close out the option position after she receives a $2 ($200) gain per contract. She doesn't use more complex options strategies, such as straddles and spreads, because these strategies depend on a stock trading within a narrow range throughout the duration of the position in order to be profitable. Most stocks move too quickly for that.

Looking to the new breed of tech stocks

Of course, holding options, calculating triggers, and closely monitoring the movements of the 50-odd stocks on her watch list can eat up a lot of a person's day. And Simon does that in addition to posting on Silicon Investor and Market Gems. "During the intense earnings season," which occurs over a period of weeks four times yearly, she says, I'm really on top of things three or four times per day." At these times Simon constantly checks her charts or scans the never-ending feed of wire stories coming from the *Wall Street Journal* News Service for anything that might affect the stocks she owns. Things relax a little the rest of the year. "Where there's only seven or eight companies that announce each week, I do it end of day."

And when she's not doing that, she's ever on the hunt for new companies to place on her watch list. Simon believes that a new breed of tech stock has emerged from the ashes of the April 2000 crash. Her revamped watch list takes into account the new, more cautious market environment. In that market, previous high flyers have become today's has-beens. And often those has-beens have become poor performers. In pre-crash times, for example, Qualcomm (QCOM) could be depended upon to rise unabated, she says. But now Simon calls it simply a day-trading stock, good for a 5-7 point gain.

Occasionally Simon allows that she'll run with the day traders if that's where she sees momentum occurring, even if it means buying into what she calls "Blimp stocks" that remain scarily overpriced (and quickly transform into lead zepelins whenever the market feels jittery). Blimps are day trades, she says, owing to their volatility. "I would not even consider keeping blimps as long-term holds. But ironically, these are the stocks that other people like. Because these are the high-profile stocks. So the minute you have a rally, people aren't going to run into IBM, they're going to run into the blimps. Whereas I would advise looking for stocks that are trading at a discount to earnings within their sector."

You can't always be short the market, and you can't always be out of the market. If you don't have a lottery ticket, you'll never win the lottery.

That less-experienced day traders want yesterday's high-flying brand-name stocks, of course, spells opportunity for her. "That's where we make our money," she says – "on the people going back in." As a result, the stocks constantly see-saw, constantly correct. In the early summer of 2000, 12 Technologies (ITWO) proved a prime example: "I could live on that stock," Simon exclaims. "It's not hard. When it's up too high it starts to waver before it begins to consolidate. And that's when I come in to short it. Or the opposite happens. It's down 14 points. And you know people are thinking that it has bottomed. The next day it's up 2 ³/₈. That's when I get in. It's up another 7 or 8 points, and I'm out again."

Those high-profit swing trades notwithstanding, Simon will tell you that she's a more conservative trader these days than she was before the crash. Her gains tend not to be as large, but they are more consistent. Longer term, like nearly all the traders profiled in this book, Simon believes the market will remain volatile, but the high-flying days are over for the foreseeable future. Though she's hardly worried. Even if the market levels off or flounders, there will still be one or two quality earnings plays per day, Simon insists. And on days when stocks go into complete arrhythmia, "I just don't get into the market," she says.

Barbara Simons's trading rules

- *Focus on accelerated quarterly earnings.* That is, earnings that rise in both percentage and real terms quarter by quarter. This is perhaps the best predictor of an explosive price move either before, during or after the actual earnings announcement.

- *Hold on to winners by loosening stops (automatic sell points).* If you get stopped out of a stock, quickly determine a profitable re-entry point.

- *Seek out so-called sleeper stocks that trade on weak technicals but forecast high earnings.*

- *Never buy stocks under $10 and don't spend more than $75 per share.* A good trade could result from a stock selling for $12-$18 per share that subsequently rises 5 or 6 percent.

- *Scalping for anything under ¹/₂ a point isn't worth the effort.* Instead look for stocks with daily price ranges of between 1 and 3 points.

- *Know a company top to bottom before you put money into it.* Study five years' worth of fundamental data especially the last 2-3 quarters, and focus especially on earnings patterns.

- *Look for profitable trades on a reversal day, which is a day where the market drops at the open, but then rises past the previous day's close.*

- *Don't hold overnight positions in "blimps" or stocks with exceptionally overinflated values.* Blimp stocks can produce decent intraday returns, since they attract hordes of momentum traders

Chapter Twelve
Long-Term Holds and
Covered Calls
Bob Martin: The Gorilla Hunter

Bob Martin began investing seriously back in April 1997. He remembers that date because it coincides exactly with the time he and his wife and the couple's two daughters bought their first home computer and hooked it to the Internet. Starting with an account worth roughly $70,000, that year Martin grew his portfolio exponentially up until the early months of 2000 when it handily topped seven figures.

True enough, the crash of 2000 had set him back by slightly more than 25 percent when we talked in the summer of 2000. But that doesn't take away from the admirable fact that Martin achieved his results largely by using a buy-and-hold strategy. Ask him; he'll tell you he probably turns over his account less than many aggressive fund managers.

Had he been a fund manager, Martin's triple-digit growth would have won him frequent invitations to appear on CNBC. But as it turns out, investing for Martin is only a part-time job. He works days as a trial lawyer, specializing in product liability cases. Moreover, his shingle hangs far from New York's financial district: in Wichita, Kansas, to be precise.

You can maybe thank that heartland city's serene atmosphere for the fact that Martin – despite the demands of his practice – can still spend 1-3 hours per day working his portfolio. "I don't know if it gives me that much more bang for the buck," he says of the time he spends. "It's become somewhat of a passion or hobby." When he's focused on his investments, Martin says he doesn't necessarily look at how the stocks he owns have traded. Instead, you'll find him reading up on technology news or trying to glean from current events just where the market's headed.

So how did a part-time buy-and-hold investor grow his portfolio from $70,000 to just over seven figures in three years? Martin will tell you that his success is all about finding stocks that are poised for hyper-growth. Those stocks – no surprise – can be found in the technology sector. Specifically, they're what Martin and traders like him all "gorilla stocks."

Gorillas in the mist

The term comes from the book *The Gorilla Game* by Geoffrey A. Moore *et al.* In simplistic terms, a gorilla stock is the biggest, most powerful beast you'll find within a given market sector. It's the company that accumulated so much proprietary technology or knowledge or muscle in some critical area that everyone must pay it tribute. Gorillas rule, in other words. And often they do so with iron hands.

> **Had he been a fund manager, Martin's triple-digit growth would have won him frequent invitations to appear on CNBC. But as it turns out, investing for Martin is only a part-time job.**

To Martin, that makes gorilla stocks the safest possible place to put his money. "Gorilla stock investing is very similar to Peter Lynch's strategy when he ran the Fidelity Magellan Fund," Martin explains. "His test was, 'Would you put more money into your stock if the stock goes down? If the answer's Yes, then that's a sign that you believe in your stock."

And when you truly believe in a stock, says Martin, you buy it and hold it and almost never let go. Martin and other gorilla stock hunters discuss possible new finds at the Silicon Investor discussion forum called Gorilla and King Portfolio Candidates.

The forum overflows with analysis about what exactly makes a gorilla stock tick. And in addition, posters name likely candidates. Recent nominations have included relatively well-known tech firms such as Phone.com (PHCM) and Real Networks (RNWK). Browse this forum and you'll also find the names of more obscure firms cropping up – companies like the Canadian graphics technology firm ATI Technologies (ATYT), or Kopin Corp. (KOPN), a maker of miniature flat-panel display screens.

All of the analysis harks back to *The Gorilla Game*, of course. The book starts off with the premise that you need some kind of framework when investing in technology stocks, or you risk losing your shirt. And the framework offered by the authors? In a nutshell, it's this simple: Certain tech stocks are destined to become the gorillas within their industry sectors. They start their ascension to the jungle throne by getting a lock on some new technology, preferably a technology the world desperately needs – whether we know it or not. As a next step, gorilla companies entice early adapters to embrace the new technology. Eventually these companies garner so much market clout they can literally force their new technology on the world. At that point, this new technology changes. The very way we live and work. Think what xerography did for office work and then for the stock of the company, Xerox, which held the patent.

Eventually, this new technology creates its own satellite economy of suppliers and channel marketers. Again, think of the firms supplying the factories churning out Intel Pentium chips, and the computer companies that implant those chips in their latest PCs.

Want another example? VCRs using the VHS standard fit the gorilla definition almost perfectly. They've enabled millions of us to time-shift our lives, recording our favourite soaps during the day while we're at work, for example, and then watching them that night. Likewise, VCRs have allowed us to capture and immediately display important moments in our lives. While at the same time they spawned a multibillion–dollar videocassette rental industry. Only recently, after reigning supreme for well over a decade, is VCR technology in danger of being supplanted by digital cameras and recordable optical disks.

If you guessed that Microsoft (MSFT) was the ultimate gorilla stock, you would be exactly right. Without question, the company rules the personal computing industry with its Windows operating system. With the exception of niche markets in graphics software and server technology, users who want to take advantage of the latest software have no choice but to build their platforms around Windows.

❝ When you truly believe in a stock, you buy it and hold it and almost never let go. ❞

Adopting an aggressive and high-margin business model similar to that used for their operating system, Microsoft also grew to dominate the markets for office suite software and Web browsers. It is only now, as the computer industry undergoes dramatic changes, that Microsoft's unrelenting hegemony is beginning to crack. The company has been unable to gain a firm foothold in businesses such as the ultra-lightweight operating systems used by pagers, personal digital assistants, and cell phones. Many people believe the future of information lies with these devices and not with desktop PCs. Nor has Microsoft secured a lock on software that would control the greatest software application of all: interactive TVs. These highly visible failures have occurred at a time when its core operating system is facing a stiff challenge from Linux. Some say that in the future the operating systems on desktop PCs will become irrelevant, as software applications and storage move increasingly to the Web.

Likewise, some might say that the Microsoft's failures have occurred in part because of its incredible successes. Customers both large and small have grown wary of a single corporation controlling so many aspects of their lives. And they've deliberately embraced alternatives. As a result, Microsoft stock, for years a veritable rock among technology issues, lost roughly half its value during 2000. The clear lesson: Even the most fearsome gorillas eventually fall. Which is why gorilla investors must constantly be on the lookout for the next big gorilla on the block.

Some of Martin's favorite gorilla stocks during the summer of 2000 included Network Appliance (NTAP) and EMC. But he especially likes a San Mateo, California, software firm called Siebel Systems (SEBL). The company has a secure niche within the fast-growing application service provider (ASP) industry. ASPs are companies that deliver software to clients either over the Internet or via some sort of private network. Housing the software in a centralized location saves the client company considerable headaches – principally, its own IT people needn't load programs individually onto thousands of company PCs. As for the ASP firm, it benefits by receiving a steady stream of revenue from clients who rent its software. Indeed, the monthly rents represent a predictable income flow. Moreover, client companies tend to stick with an ASP once they sign on, since the costs of a changeover would be prohibitive. For these reasons, Martin believes Siebel is a classic gorilla company in the making. It has the high margins typical of a software provider, and it has a lock on its customers.

Housekeeping chores

Needless to say, other gorilla stocks in the making await discovery. To hedge his bets, Martin follows the advice of the *Gorilla Game* authors. "I group the stocks I own into different baskets or sectors," he says. "Then I will scan through to see if the stocks are all reacting the same that particular day." Martin says he checks on his baskets daily. "What I'm trying to see," he explains, "is how that sector did and if any of the stocks have gone down or up. Or if the sector overall has done well or badly for the day." The basket system is designed to reveal which of the stocks possess the best chance for long-term success. Grooming a portfolio essentially entails trimming back on losers and adding to your winners.

But how does Martin decide when it's time to make specific changes? "If there's one stock that's really gone up, or really gone down," he says, "I'll zoom in on that and take a look at what's going on. If it's going up too much, maybe I should take some profits, or maybe I should put more money into it. Anytime you get a stock that is going vertically, you cannot sustain it too long."

He's less inclined to sell off stocks he considers true gorillas. Because, he explains, "a gorilla stock is going to have a lot of staying power to it. So there's no guarantee that you'll be able to buy it again at a lower price."

To time his trades more precisely, Martin has begun using candlestick charts. He also uses bar charts and Bollinger bands. The latter indicator frames a stock's price chart and depicts the potential trading range at each new price point.

And what if the stock's going down? How much pain will he endure before exiting? Martin tries to fathom the reasons for the decline before making a move. He also admits to second-guessing himself. "Should I have put a stop loss?" he'll ask himself. "Should I get out of it or should I just hold on?"

Theory and practice of stop loss orders

Active traders have strong opinions about stop orders. Stop loss orders automatically close out a position if the shares fall to a predetermined price. Some insist stops are essential to protect profits. Others say they're a sure way to lock in a loss. Martin leans more toward the latter group, particularly with technology stocks. First off, there's the volatility. A stock might easily sink during a bad day of trading only to rise back to its opening price. But there's another, perhaps more sinister reason why Martin and other traders believe stops are a bad idea. "The information about where your stop loss is contained within the computer systems at the brokerage houses, and so all the broker dealers know where your stops are." It's possible in other words, for the broker dealers to walk a stock down to its stop level in order to trigger a sell, and then run the stock back up on you. "I've been nicked too many times where I just barely get stopped and then the stock is up by 10 points by the end of the day or the end of the week."

Under what circumstances would he resort to using stops? "If I had a large enough position where I was concerned about preserving profit, then I might," he says. "If I do that, I'm looking at a good 15 to 25 percent drop before triggering the stop. The stop's not tight because the volatility's so great."

Still, he clearly understands that as a position deteriorates the chances of his recouping his loss decline. Do the math: If a stock drops by 50 percent, he explains, it must double in price before the loss is made up. A 60 percent drop requires something like a 150 percent gain to recover.

Some traders average down to help ease their losses. But Martin believes this only exacerbates losses. You have to do the opposite. "You have to put more money into the winners and cut the losers and be done with it," he says. "It's called "the Russian Army approach." In World War II," Martin explains, "the Russian generals would give supplies to their armies based on how well they did. If the armies did well, they would get more supplies. If they didn't, the generals would starve them."

Covered call writing

But even when adding to winning positions, Martin seldom owns more than 500 shares of a given stock. In fact, he likes to buy and sell in round lots because this enables him to put another risk-reducing strategy to work – a strategy that can also generate substantial income: covered call option writing.

"People come to options in one of two ways," Martin says. "One is they want to make money, so they get into buying calls and then they lose it all. The second way is they accumulate money and they buy the stock. At some point it dawns on them that they ought to sell the covered calls for the added income. That's the way I've come." And instead of losing money, he says, he's created a more or less predictable income stream from the strategy. Notwithstanding the profits that can be made, covered call writing is probably the most conservative options strategy. So conservative, in fact, that most brokerages permit you to sell covered calls even within a tax-deferred retirement account such as an IRA.

Here's how the strategy works: When you sell or "write" a covered call you're actually giving someone else the option to purchase the stock from you at an agreed-upon price, called the "strike price." The call is considered covered because you already own the underlying stock. If the call is exercised, you simply hand over those shares. Contrast that with so-called naked call writing, a far more dangerous strategy. When you sell naked calls, the absolute last thing you want to have happen is for the stock to rise significantly in price. And for an obvious reason: The price rise will result in the call being exercised. And it will obligate you to purchase the stock at whatever its current market price happens to be. Then you must sell it at whatever the call's strike price happened to be – even if this means a significant loss.

Back to covered call writing. Why would anyone want to hand over stock that might possibly rise in price? For a couple of reasons, it turns out. In some cases, investors may have owned the stock for years, and they now believe they've received as much gain from it as possible. In other cases, people buy the underlying stock with the sole objective of using it as a vehicle for writing covered calls. Here's an example: Let's say you buy 100 shares of a reasonably volatile stock. Because the stocks volatile you can expect to receive a premium from the call sale equal to – let's say – 5 percent of the stock's current price. So, for example, if you bought CMGI (a volatile stock if ever there was one) for 20 and then sold a call that was 30 days from expiration, a call that also had a strike price of 20, the $1 premium you received would work out to a 5 percent profit for the one month before the call's expiration. If CMGI rose to over 20, the call would be considered "in the money," and would likely be exercised, meaning you could expect a call from your broker informing you of your obligation to turn over the shares. If CMGI fell to 18, however, the call would expire worthless. And the 5 percent profit you received from the call sale would help repay some of that decline. Also, you would then be free to sell another call. And the premium from the second call would likely more than make up for the remainder of your loss.

You can also finesse this strategy by varying the strike price. If you expect CMGI to go from 20 to 25 in the time period between now and the call's expiration date, you might sell a call with a strike price of 25. If your prediction proved correct, this would significantly increase your profits from the trade. It would allow you to receive 5 points from the gain in the stock's price plus the premium from the call you sold.

In the money

When writing calls on gorilla stocks, Martin often chooses a strategy that's completely opposite from the one just described. "One of the best strategies is to sell-in-the-money covered calls," he says. In-the-money calls have strike prices below the stock's current market price. If XYZ stock's selling for $60, for example, an in-the-money call might have a strike price of $55. The price received for the call would be $5, plus an added premium for time value. If ABC were an especially volatile stock, the $55 strike call with a 30-day expiration might sell for $6, with $5 of that denoting intrinsic value and $1 representing time value. People often sell in-the-money calls when the market is especially volatile. And it's easy to see why: If XYZ stock were to decline to 50, as a call writer you'd still earn $1 just by holding the stock for one month. As you can see, writing an in-the-money call can give you considerable downside protection.

Here's how Martin says the strategy works for him: Let's say I have 500 shares of Siebel. I'll sell five contracts in the money by about $5 or $10, so I have some time value, but I also have some share value [i.e., intrinsic value]. And that gives me greater downside protection. I fully intend to be called out. I've sold covered calls in Siebel with a strike price of 155 when the stock was a $162. And I made about $7,000. I'm happy. I've made 10 percent in a month. The only negative is when the stocks keep running up like Siebel does, you get a little depressed. But you have to be in tune with the fact that you're using the stock as a tool, as means to make the money."

Siebel Systems, which was selling at over $102 at the time of this writing and with a P/E ratio north of 280, is a relatively expensive stock. But Martin says price rarely enters into the equation when he's choosing stocks for his covered call writing. "I've owned SDLI [optical equipment maker SDL Inc.], which has been up to over $400 per share. And that's fine. For covered call writing, my focus is on percentages. I really don't care what the price of the underlying stock is."

The percentage return varies with the call's expiration date. Calls with the highest annualized percentage returns are usually 4-6 weeks from expiration. But as Martin explains, other factors come into play when selecting an expiration date for the call he sells. "Usually the expiration I choose is one month," he says. "I'm starting to think about going a little further out, to 1½ months to 2 months. Just because of the volatility. You've got a little more time to react and buy back the covered call if you want to."

Call writing risks

Martin brings up a good point. Covered call positions can go bad in one or two ways. If the stock greatly increases in price, you miss out on that profit opportunity. More ominously, the stock might crash. If that happens, the call premium will certainly offset some of your loss. But not all of it. Repairing the damage in either case involves repurchasing the call you originally sold and perhaps selling another call in its place. This strategy is known as "rolling down" or "rolling out." When rolling down a call, you buy back your original call. If the stock's gone down in price, the call will be cheaper as well. Once you've closed out your call position by buying back your original call, you can sell another call with a lower strike price. Rolling out a call also involves re-purchasing your original call to close out the position. Then you sell another call with an expiration date that's further out. The further out the expiration date, the more time value that's incorporated in the call's price. And that time value, of course, translates into a higher premium. It's possible to combine a rolling down and rolling out strategy to further boost the call premiums you receive. And you can apply a variation of the strategy if the stock price rises significantly and you want to keep a portion of that gain.

Gorilla companies are leading us into a future in which everything people do can be done more efficiently and more productively. There's a synergistic effect, where connectivity is happening. They're actually part of the economy, and they're leading us forward.

But Martin says he's had a few bad experiences with each strategy. "When walking [i.e. rolling] calls up," he says, "the big negative is you don't want to put more money into the stock. So I'm actually walking it up and out. Walking it up in strike price and walking it out too fast. On the downside, I have rolled down a call, and you get caught locking yourself into a loss."

Another risk with covered call writing is having your call exercised before the expiration date. Under the American-style rules, options can be redeemed at any time up until the last trading day before they expire. In other words, at any moment you might receive that fateful call from your broker, instructing you to hand over your shares.

But Martin says this danger is largely overstated. "You hardly ever get called out of these things prior to expiration. The reason," he theorizes "is that options are used as a trading mechanism rather than an investing mechanism. People buy the options and then sell them later at a higher price. Or they sell the covered call to have it expire worthless, or then buy it back cheaply and sell another one. Hardly anyone buys calls to actually exercise them and buy the underlying stocks. There's so much buying back and forth that there's a lot of liquidity. So you can really run the call right up to the day of expiration. If expiration arrives and the shares are in the money, you automatically get called out. But you have until that day to buy back the call and sell another one."

Income for life

So what does Martin do if his shares do get called out? "Pick another stock," he says, "and do the same thing. Or repurchase a smaller quantity of the original stock (that's gone up). And sell another covered call. I'll pick the same stock over and over again if from a technical analysis standpoint it's worthwhile to do."

Martin maintains a list of 10-20 stocks he uses for covered call writing. He especially likes gorilla stocks because he's bullish on them long term. Even if they fall in price while he's waiting for the call to expire, he can feel assured they will eventually recover. And meanwhile, there are all those monthly premium checks to cash from his call writing.

"If you were an investor who strongly believed in the company," he says "you might sell covered calls that were out of the money to reduce the risk of getting called out but still earning premium income." However, some covered call writers are interested solely in the income potential. "A trader who's position trading or day trading or swing trading sees the stock as a tool. They couldn't care less about the stock or its story. They're just using the stock as a way of making money." As Martin explains, "A good covered call strategy in that context would be to buy a gorilla stock, since you should like the stock if you're going to write a covered call. Then constantly milk the money out of successive covered calls. And then just add the money back in and keep doing it. For example, if I buy 500 shares of Siebel and then I sell five covered calls, I may make $5,000 to $10,000. I could then take that premium and buy 100 shares of Network Appliance and sell another covered call on that, and then put that premium into another stock."

Call it pyramiding your profits, or the miracle of compound interest. Martin believes covered call writing will make up at least a third of his investment gains in the years ahead. The rest of that income will come from winners within his baskets of gorilla stocks. He hopes someday to amass a large enough portfolio to scale back his legal work. "I enjoy helping my legal clients," Martin says. "But it's a lot of work. My work is litigation work, so when you see people they're in a bad mood whether they're a plaintiff or a defendant. Investing is a lot more fun. The consequences are entirely my own. Therefore the result is something I can live with."

Bob Martin's trading rules

Gorilla stocks

- *Don't diversify into seemingly safe areas such as bonds and utilities.* You only succeed in diversifying yourself into mediocre returns.

- *Do diversify within technology sectors.* A portfolio might include blue-chip gorilla stocks and stocks you expect will become gorilla stocks in the future. The stocks should represent all the important areas of technology such as fiber optics, storage, semiconductors, and wireless communications. Choose dominant companies within those sectors. Also choose companies that appear to be expanding their revenues. A certain amount of the portfolio should be reserved for cash to allow for new opportunities.

- *Find the gorilla.* The safest place in the world to invest is in growing companies that are leading the economy forward. "The companies that embrace change the quickest are the safest because they can turn on a dime," says Martin, "versus a dinosaur company that doesn't know what they're doing and can't respond."

- *Group stocks you own into different baskets or sectors.* Then scan those baskets daily to see if the stocks are all reacting the same for that particular day. Study how each basket or sector did and if any of its component stocks have gone down or up by an unusual amount. Understand the reasons behind any significant price changes.

- *Use the "Peter Lynch test":* If you thoroughly believe in a stock, you'll put more money into it, even if its experiences a short-term price decline.

- *Devise an entry and exit strategy for each stock you own.* In other words, determine the prices at which you'll buy in or sell. Consider this information a kind of mental stop, and use it in lieu of sending an actual stop loss order to your broker. If you do set actual stops, especially on volatile tech stocks, give the stock plenty of leeway – say 15-25 percent.

- *Take profits on gorilla stocks only when the stock is rising on a steep curve.* Repurchase the stock during the inevitable retracement.

- *Limit the size of individual trades.* Try not to buy or sell any more than 200 shares at a time. Study the typical size of trades before buying and try to stay within these parameters so your trades don't attract attention.

Covered call writing

- *Focus on percentage gains and not the price of the stock.*

- *View stocks primarily as a tool for making money via call writing and not as a long-term investment.*

- *Stagger the covered calls you write.* As Martin explains, "If I have 300 shares of Siebel Systems, I could sell one covered call in the money, one at the money, and one out of the money. So I'd have a blend. And then based on the volatility I might want to buy back one or more of the calls. That way I'd have some capital appreciation if the stock goes up, and I 'd have some risk avoidance if it goes down."

- *Maintain a watch list of stocks you wish to use for covered call writing.* Thoroughly research the prospects of the companies beforehand.

- *Sell in-the-money calls for added downside protection if markets appear especially volatile.*

- *Repurchase the calls if the stock declines.* Sell new ones with lower strike prices and lengthier expiration dates.

- *Wait until the last possible moment to buy back calls that have not been exercised.* Because options incorporate time value in their pricing, their value diminishes as they approach their expiration date. Therefore, you can often buy back the call for less than you originally paid, and prevent the shares from being exercised from your portfolio.

- *Compound your winnings.* If your call option is exercised, you can pick another stock and write calls on it. Alternately, you can buy a smaller quantity of the original stock (since it has gone up in price) and write an appropriate number of covered calls.

Chapter Thirteen
If I Only Had a Brain...
Scott McCormick: The AI Guy

Take yourself back for a moment to the mid-'80s, that good-time era of corporate raiders and wallowing S&Ls. The economy's humming along. The stock market's been jolted from the doldrums by steady infusions of IRA cash. And institutional money managers everywhere are looking for some new kind of tool that'll help them whup their peers. Who do they turn to for help but a bunch of math, physics, and computer wizards, nerds in the classic sense, who for years have laboured away in dismal academic posts dabbling in arcane areas like LISP, Learning vector quantization and Kohonan architecture. Like rogue governments courting Russian nuclear scientists, the institutional funds seduced, then sequestered their prized academics in the funds' back offices. There, these so-called quants or rocket scientists set to work in secret. Their quest could be summed up simply: Find that Holy Grail of computer algorithms that can predict markets. Make us rich!

To accomplish their task, many of the scientists turned to a little-known kind of computer program called a "neural net." Unlike traditional software, neural nets can actively learn from past experience and apply those lessons to entirely new situations: veritable thinking machines, in other words, modeled after the way we human beings ourselves think!

The story continues. These scientists were in fact wildly successful in their quest. When one institution's scientist shouted "Eureka!" at an impending uptrend, the other institutions' scientists – all working independently, of course – shouted "Eureka!" too. Neural nets back in those days were all very similar. So they tended to behave the same way.

Even though the institutional managers were largely clueless as to how these newfangled neural nets worked, they eagerly heeded the programs'

❝ Unlike traditional software, neural nets can actively learn from past experience and apply those lessons to entirely new situations: veritable thinking machines, in other words, modeled after the way we human beings ourselves think! **❞**

recommendations. Accordingly, billions of dollars moved in and out of markets.

Not surprisingly, the markets went into arrhythmia as a result. Then, near the end of October 1987, so the story goes, neural nets all across the country signalled as one that a little profit taking was called for. Sell orders flew from trading rooms. The selling snowballed. Panic ensued, visions of doom, *voila*: Black Monday ....

Creepy science

No one really knows how much neural nets really contributed to the October crash, if at all. But the story does point to the aura of mystery and intrigue that has always surrounded neural nets. The rumors and stories that circulate about the software have a *Weekly World News* quality to them. Did a neural network smuggled into a Las Vegas casino really beat the house at roulette? Do Swiss bankers have a computer hidden in the basement somewhere that guides them in pillaging world markets? Does the Defense Department possess a neural net that – get this – has actually developed self-awareness?

Trading from his home in the Michigan suburbs, Scott McCormick enjoys the mystique surrounding neural nets. And indeed, he's had a hand in creating some of it. In the course of his career, he's helped design software for NASA's deep space probes. And he's spearheaded black-box projects for the Defense Department. "We did a lot of man-machine interface, what I call a 'dialogical interface,'" he says, describing this top-secret work. In layman's terms, that means he and his team were looking for ways to communicate with their artificially intelligent software. "A lot of that work's classified. All I can say is that there were some tremendous successes and some dismal failures."

With degrees in mathematics and aerospace engineering and a minor in theoretical physics, McCormick's been utilizing neural networks for 12 years. And for 9 of those years he's put the software to work on his own investment portfolio. The first thing he'll tell you is that neural nets aren't the Holy Grail. "All a neural net does is identify a pattern," McCormick says. "They [the designers] can put a lot of front ends on it to make it look like it does everything else. But all it does is pattern matching." Sounds logical. Think about it. If someone actually possessed a program that could predict the markets with killer accuracy, they would own the planet by now.

That said, placed in the right hands, neural networks can produce a return that's not at all shabby. While McCormick doesn't like to talk about the specific results of his personal investments, he claims to have taken over seven figures from the markets over the years. And in large part, that's been with the help of neural nets. More astounding, he claims his returns, largely derived from position trading and long-term holds, have never fallen below 50 percent annually. "The year that I kept best track of it, I made 137 trades, averaged 5 percent per trade. My worst failures came from not setting proper stops. When I failed to apply that discipline, I've lost as much as 100 grand."

More astounding still, like several other traders in this book, McCormick's achieved these results throughout the market's ups and downs, and he did it while employed at some fairly high-pressured jobs. Currently, he's director of operations for Peak Industries, a Dearborn, Michigan, computer-based design and proto-typing firm with close ties to the auto industry. The job routinely requires him to put in 12-hour days. Then again, this is a guy who started pursing a mathematics degree at the University of Wisconsin when he was 14. "People tend to shy away from you at cocktail parties when you tell them that," he says.

Besides investing, McCormick's other projects include several Web sites. One is called Neural101.com, a site he helps manage with colleague Daniel Ervi, a computer programmer/investor who's based in Canada. Neural101.com, as its name implies, is intended to teach other investors the rudiments of neural nets. An even more ambitious project, which McCormick was still in the process of tweaking when we talked, is Fundpilot.com. Intended as a subscription site, Fundpilot.com is McCormick's attempt to use neural networks to generate buy and sell signals for mutual fund portfolios.

> **" Even though the institutional managers were largely clueless as to how these newfangled neural nets worked, they eagerly heeded the programs' recommendations. Accordingly, billions of dollars moved in and out of markets. "**

The two-tiered screening system

So how does he find time to invest? A disciplined schedule, to be sure, McCormick says he spends 16-18 hours per week perusing his portfolio. But he's greatly aided by the half-dozen or so computers that are networked together throughout the home he and wife share. "Everything I've got set up is structured so that I get the information I need," he says. "My analysis is at night." That analysis entails running stocks through two distinct software applications. The first screens stocks based on technical indicators. And it's similar to, although far more granular than, the stock screens you'll find at free financial sites all over the Web. Using the results from this screen, McCormick creates a shorter list. He then reanalyzes most of the stocks using a neural net, comparing the results of the two. Using this information, McCormick then sets target prices for certain key stocks. And these targets take the form of limit orders that he might enter the following day.

The whole process starts with a watch list that McCormick has continually groomed over the years. "I generally keep around 300 stocks in the portfolio that I screen," McCormick says. "I change what's on the list no more often than every quarter. Some companies merge. Some drop below certain volume limits. Or they're just a flash in the pan. Out of the 300 there are probably 220 that are technology stocks, including biotechnology." The remainder, McCormick says, might be anything from financial stocks to retail. McCormick likes to focus on sector leaders. And so his portfolio includes, for example, all the sector leaders within Internet stocks. His watch list also includes all 30 stocks that make up the Dow.

> "All a neural net does is identify a pattern," McCormick says. "The designers can put a lot of front ends on it to make it look like it does everything else. But all it does is pattern matching."

Occasionally, McCormick will add an IPO to his list. "Martha Stewart from the moment it IPOed was worth watching for the reversal," he says. "I knew it was going to come at some point. The problem with IPOs is that people stop looking after a month or two, and it generally reverses well after that, once the market flushes out the people who bought too high and couldn't stand to hold it. Once you've taken advantage of that reversal, the stock will establish itself at some price. In the case of Martha Stewart I think it ran from 58 to 30, so that was a worthwhile opportunity. But after that if it doesn't go anywhere, based on fundamental analysis I may choose not to follow it anymore."

Indicator drift

So sometime after dinner each night, the hard drives on McCormick's computers squawk and grunt in the downstairs of his home as the programs look at each stock's recent market performance. "I do all of my technical analysis on a Mac using a product called ProTA." It's worth noting that ProTA (www.beesoft.net) is one of the few high-end financial programs designed to run on a Mac. And for that reason, perhaps, it's acquired a kind of cult following. "The graphics are much better on a Mac," explains McCormick.

Specifically, he says a Mac processes graphical information much faster than a PC, which means you can rapidly skim from chart to chart. "I know a couple of people who download a couple of thousand stocks every night, and they have some pretty rigorous screens."

> **While McCormick doesn't like to talk about the specific results of his personal investments, he claims to have taken over seven figures from the markets over the years. And in large part, that's been with the help of neural nets.**

McCormick says he likes to screen using a fairly hefty number of indicators. And sometimes he must adjust those indicators to compensate for changes in market conditions. That's because of something McCormick calls "indicator drift." Think of the dial on an analog radio that you must continually adjust in order to pick up far-off stations. For example, he says, "If I was using a stochastic and after a while it began failing to be an indicator of a significant price change, I realized that – okay – there was something going on." Years back, when markets were somewhat more peaceful in nature, it took 9 months before whatever set of indicators McCormick happened to be using quit doing their job. Nowadays, that time frame's shortened to 2-3 months, he says.

"I've never been able to figure out why indicator drift occurs," says McCormick. The researcher part of his psyche once compelled him to undertake a study of various stocks, comparing their performance to the buzz they generated on the Web's myriad financial chat sites. The results were inconclusive, he says.

Notwithstanding, indicator drift can punish traders. "It's like CANSLIM," McCormick says. He's referring to the wildly popular investment strategy devised by William O'Neil, the founder of *Investor's Business Daily*. CANSLIM is an acronym for a kind of detailed stock screen detailed in O'Neil's book *How to Make Money in Stocks.* The screen incorporates indicators such as quarterly earnings, new products, leadership within the sector, institutional sponsorship, and market direction. "Everyone will tell you CANSLIM worked great in 1997-1998 and then just died when the market took off in late '98 and '99," says McCormick. "Same thing with Elliott Wave Theory." Here McCormick's referring to a popular technical charting strategy. "No one can tell you what waves you're in until after it's occurred. That's not real useful."

Faced with the prospect of indicators routinely failing on him, McCormick did what any good engineer might do: He built lots of redundancy into his trading system – meaning he created a large arsenal of indicators that he could draw from.

Yet, even a large set of indicators requires tweaking and at time some strategic decisions on McCormick's part. "If the indicators were no longer working for that particular stock, the choice is do I get rid of that particular stock or develop a method for just that stock? Since the stock universe is so large," McCormick says there's little reason to customize screens for just one stock. Except, perhaps, for widely held stocks like Coca-Cola. "Coke will go up and down fairly regularly and it was fairly easy to take a position in. And then I noticed that it reached a plateau and started oscillating and getting narrower and narrower in range. And from my reading I knew that that was pretty much when people started abandoning it and going on to whatever the new thing was."

Getting neural

At the end of part one of the evening's number crunching, McCormick's ProTA software spits out about 20 stocks – sometimes more, sometimes less – any one of which might be poised for a significant move in one direction or another. To confirm those potential movements, or if he simply wants a crack at spotting entirely different opportunities, McCormick next runs an analysis through his neural net. The program he uses, called NeuroShell Trader from Ward Systems (www.wardsystems.com), is actually a template that McCormick can customize depending on what he's looking for. The program lets you scroll through some 800 pre-programmed technical indicators – things like percent change at close, one-month moving average, and volume gain. Select those indicators you normally follow when analyzing a stock. NeuroShell automatically downloads financial data from the Web, then tests it with the indicators you've chosen. "You can take the moving average of the linear regression of a stochastic if you want. It's that robust of a programming language that's available to you," says McCormick.

But there is a danger of overkill. "The package systems can let you spend all your time doing analysis and none of your time actually coming up with an answer," he says. Generally, "you're not looking for a general market pattern; you're looking at that pattern for a particular stock." And the reason for that, he says, is that "a stock is owned generally by the same kinds of people, or by the same funds with generally the same objectives. And it's the volume of ownership that really drives where the stock is going to move. A classic example is Microsoft (MSFT). Microsoft used to have 80 percent institutional ownership. By the time everybody got done selling it, it was down to 40 percent institutional ownership. About then was when everybody realized that the price was dropping."

A mind of its own

Okay, so when you use a neural net you're looking for a pattern. But specifically how do neural nets recognize and then alert you to those patterns it considers significant? Here is a short course.

Neural networks come from the ethereal realm of computer science called "artificial intelligence." Or AI for short. Other AI areas include so-called genetic algorithms and fuzzy logic. Genetic algorithms mimic the forces of evolution by breeding and mutating in an effort to achieve an answer to a problem. Fuzzy logic allows programs to discern gray areas within a sea of data, rather than the simple plus/minus, on/off, and $^0/_1$ of traditional binary processing. Both genetic algorithms and fuzzy logic have been incorporated into neural nets.

Today, unknown to most people, the software is in fact commonly used. Applications can be found anywhere a degree of judgment is called for. For example, banks use neural nets to scope through your credit history and determine whether or not you should be approved for a home loan. Database search programs use them to find pictures or photographs – faces are if nothing else patterns. And indeed, companies are experimenting with neural nets that will recognize facial expressions and thereby sense your mood.

Calling neural nets lifelike is not much of a stretch, either. McCormick recalls a sophisticated neural net used by the Defense Department for certain unspecified black-box projects. The program developed a rudimentary form of self-awareness, says McCormick. "It's self-aware in the fact that it recognizes elements that are new to its environment," he says. "If it encounters an issue that it doesn't know how to deal with, it works to understand how to deal with it."

McCormick was able to recount one particularly eerie incident involving this self-aware neural net: "We removed the optical sensors from it [the program] and it came back after about two days and asked in mathematical form, 'why do I fear the dark?' It was asking why it was hesitant to do things that didn't require an optical input," McCormick explains. "That's really about all I can tell you."

Despite all the hype and mystery, the nuts and bolts behind neural nets are disarmingly simple. In essence neurals seek to define the relationship between independent variables and a dependent variable – create a kind of workable equation in other words.

The process consists of a few simple steps. First, feed it a range of data. It could be the number and size of sunspots along with temperature and humidity of Earth and then a succession of wheat futures prices. Regardless, the neural will seek to find a relationship. Alternately you could look at the high, low, and closing price of a stock, along with its daily volume. Again, the software will try to discern a relationship.

How, specifically? This data gets entered into a spreadsheet. The better programs handle this seamlessly. The high, low, close, and volume make up the equation's independent variables. The dependent variable – the thing you're trying to predict – is the following day's closing price.

Extracting this information from the spreadsheet, the neural network goes to work. First it generates a neuron (a mini-number cruncher) for each of the variables, and an additional neuron for the output. The network assigns "weights" to describe the influence each independent variable has on the dependent variable. Is the high, the low, or the close of greatest influence on the closing price, and by how much?

The network then goes about testing the variables over a sample period. For example, it might look at the high, low, close, and volume over a one-month period. Using historical pricing data, it will attempt to predict an outcome based on the weight it has assigned. Then it will compare its prediction to the actual answer. As it proceeds, the network, adjusts the weights of the variables with the goal of improving its accuracy. In the process, it may create additional "hidden" neurons, to better crunch the data. Hidden neurons may link two or more variable neurons together and create a third link to the output. Additional weights are assigned to these links. In this way the network becomes increasingly complex. The process continues until the network's predictions closely mirror the actual answers.

In the next stage, what's called "forward testing" begins. That is, new data gets fed into the network. High, low, and close figures from the previous five days get fed in, for example, in an effort to predict tomorrow's closing price. Now the network gets to show off how well it's learned.

Sometimes networks over-train. That is, they learn the relationship to their old data so well that they can't adapt this knowledge to new and different situations. Sort of like a life-time student of Beethoven who can't play a lick of jazz.

That analogy isn't so farfetched. The way the neurons adjust the weight of the information they receive is analogous to the way millions of nerve cells in our brains strive to work in concert to enable us to learn to hit a fastball pitch or speak fluent Mandarin.

Bugs in the system

Some newer neural networks incorporate what are known as "genetic algorithms" as a way of increasing their effectiveness. Genetic algorithms represent yet another AI foray modeled on the way life works, in this case the cruel forces of Darwinian selection. Like tiny microbes in a lab dish, genetic algorithms live or die based on their ability to perform a desired function. The survivors breed and mutate until – let's say – a potent new strain of stock predictors gets created.

Sometimes genetic algorithms are embedded within neural networks, in which case they work to adjust the weights of the links between neurons. Other times, like electronic leeches, the algorithms can be programmed to attach themselves to hundreds, even thousands of separate neural networks all deconstructing the same problem. The genetic algorithms kill off those networks that don't pass muster, breeding new strains of better predictors in the process.

It sounds like a sci-fi premise: the thinking ability of the human brain, the breeding capacity of a virus. And they're running amuck through the world's financial markets!

Disappearing scientists

Scott McCormick got up to speed with neural networks when he developed a program to help guide a satellite as it left our solar system. "When a satellite goes outside our solar system it goes outside the realm of normal Newtonian physics," he explains. *Ergo*, the need for artificially intelligent software to help navigate in this totally alien environment. In the course of his work for NASA, McCormick got to thinking about how neurals might be applied to finance. "I did a very detailed analysis," he says. "I knew of people who were working on neurals for major funds. Somewhat back in time, the individual would publish two or three major works and then he wouldn't publish any more. I'd call the university and find out he'd left. Is there some kind of conspiracy there that they're keeping it quiet?"

Little by little word has seeped out. In March 1993, for example, the magazine *U.S. News & World Report* reported on how LBS Capital Management in Safety Harbor, Florida, used a neural program to beat the S&P 500 by 24 percent annually for six years running. In July 1994, *Wired* magazine featured a group of computer-savvy hippies fresh from a commune who had devised a computer small enough to fit in a shoe. The toes acted as a keyboard. And the computer indicated its answers by tapping back at the bottom of the wearer's foot. The group smuggled their invention into a Las Vegas casino, where it predicted winning numbers at roulette – well enough to beat the house. The former commune members reportedly then went to work applying high-end math to the financial world. *Wired* magazine and *New Yorker* writer Thomas A. Bass has chronicled the adventures of these techno-savvy merry pranksters in his book *The Predictors*.

If it looks like an elephant and acts like an elephant, it must be an elephant

All heady stuff, to be sure. So are neurals really that good? "For $1,000 you can put in a neural net and it'll tell you exactly when a stock should go up but never why it didn't," McCormick jokes. He views neurals as a tool. And as tools they have their place, just as stock screening tools have their place. "A screening tool is great for screening for things you want to look at," he says. He relies on his technical screens to confirm when to exit a stock. Neural nets by contrast are better at confirming entry points. "I'm tending to use the strengths of both of them," he says.

"But it's really all in how you develop the net," says McCormick. "You can develop a net that's specifically geared toward when you should get in. The problem is people tend to use whatever they use to get in and then reverse it to get out. That's where most people tend to fail."

Not that you need to be a rocket scientist to master neural nets. McCormick claims that anyone with a little knowledge of statistics and good market savvy can use the software – and without understanding a lick of programming. As McCormick says, neurals "won't make a bad trader good." But they can "make a good trader better." First you need to know "what kind of things influence price," he adds. Otherwise using a neural net's "like having a router. If you don't know what a router does, having one's not going to help you.

"I know a tobacco farmer who's very good at it," McCormick says. Like other non-techies who successfully use neurals, he says, the farmer uses one of the many off-the-shelf neural programs currently available that are no more difficult to program than a spreadsheet.

The secret lies in how you present your data sample to the net. McCormick explains: "If you give a neural net a lot of information about a very small number of items, it can make a pattern recognition or prediction that it will tell you has a huge confidence level, 90 percent. But it'll be wrong."

To illustrate, suppose you told a computer program everything there was to know about an elephant. Then you presented the net with new data – a mouse. Because of its learning, the net would reason that it had encountered a very small elephant. On the other hand, if you described a few critical attributes of all the mammals on Earth and then showed the neural net a mouse, the program would likely surmise it was dealing with some kind of rodent.

Translated into the financial arena: Present just a few indicators – such as high, low, close, volume at close, for example – but enter this data for a great many days. Once the neural net digests this information – often this takes just a matter of minutes – the real fun begins: Retesting the computer on the real thing. McCormick suggests paper trading with your system for about a month before putting cash on the line.

Years from now, maybe everyone will use neurals to help manage their investments. "Neurals will help accelerate panic and exuberance and eventually equalize markets," predicts McCormick. He notes, "The first individual investors using neural nets in the early '90s were equalized out in a couple of years." So much for those market inefficiencies. To ferret out opportunities in the future, McCormick believes investors will have to look to exotic markets. Several years ago he designed a neural net to study volatile Indonesian securities – so far with less than complete success. "The start of the monsoon season will influence their markets," he says. "And that I don't know how to account for."

Scott McCormick's trading rules

- *Don't focus on the opening or closing price of a stock.* Rather try to "discover the trading range for the following day."

- *Volume is a poor indicator of a stock's future price.* "I've never found volume to be particularly indicative of anything."

- *Let the market come to you.* Set limit entries and exits based on your analysis. If the market fails to reach your predetermined level, wait for another opportunity.

- *Use Neurals to look at patterns for particular stocks rather than general market patterns.* Stocks exhibit patterns because the individuals and institutions that own them have similar goals, and therefore tend to trade in similar fashion.

- *Use stops.* "If you don't set the stop, you're going to be a long-term investor until the company goes broke."

Conclusion
A Master List of Trading Rules

If there's one paramount, indelible truth the traders in this book can teach us, it's that an average intelligent person can indeed succeed at trading. In an upbeat market they can grow their portfolios to substantial sums. And they can do it in a relatively short time. Granted, four of the people interviewed, namely Teresa Lo, Oliver Velez, Chris Farrell, and Brendan DeLamielleure, had worked previously as professional traders. So you could say they brought along some valuable experience when they set out on their own. And true enough, their results were for the most part better, or at least more consistent, than those of the rank amateurs (more about this later). You could also claim, correctly, that all 12 traders benefited immeasurably from the unprecedented bull market of 1998-2000. Still, their return rates far exceeded those of the average trader. Strategy played a crucial role.

For that very reason the strategies these 12 traders used to succeed during that bull market can surely serve as lessons for the rest of us. There will always be a bull market over the horizon, no matter how bearish things might seem at any given time. And, though the names of the companies leading the new bull stampede will seem unfamiliar and untested, the best investors will naturally be those who recognize these new emerging companies. And using tested tactics, these successful investors will be able to exploit early moves in those stocks.

Just as there always will be bull markets, there will also inevitably be choppy, bearish, and dangerously volatile markets. And this is the area where the traders profiled in this book can perhaps teach us the most. Because at the end of the day, the most successful investors will not necessarily be those who've raked in the most. Rather it will be those who were able to preserve their gains during the market's downward spirals. With perhaps one or two exceptions, all

12 traders weathered the April 2000 crash with the bulk of their portfolios intact. And, as noted, some were able to continue growing their portfolios to new highs, even as the rest of us watched our losses mount.

Let's, then, take a look at the tactics that appear to have served these 12 traders best – particularly those tactics the majority seemed to have in common. From there we can examine something that is perhaps far harder to define – namely, those common personality traits that contributed to each of the 12 investors' successes.

The master list: 14 trading rules

Rule number 1: Start slow

Sounds like common sense. Without question, if you leap headlong into the market, and you don't take the time to receive proper training, you're going to crash and burn. Depend on it. Remember Terry Bruce? He rode his $75,000 in life savings up to $575,000, only to see his account slip back down to zero. His gains came from picking high-momentum stocks that many other beginning traders just like him were likewise piling into. A little training might have shown him how to spot a top and how to exit. Second time around, when Bruce got a stake together, he did his homework. And he traded far more conservatively – and with better results.

> **"Trading conservatively, using small amounts of cash, is especially important after suffering a setback. "**

Five traders in this book – Farrell, DeLamielleure, Lo, Simon, and Velez – all told me they tended to trade conservatively in the sense that they followed exacting rules and worked to keep their risk exposure to a minimum. Again, remember that these, with the exception of Simon were the most experienced of the lot, having spent years working as professional traders before going out on their own. Velez was perhaps best at defining the rules he traded by, rules that enabled him to exit positions with better assurance of a gain. Farrell traded extremely conservative debt instruments that barely budged in price. And he too had specific rules governing what issues he would trade and under what conditions. DeLamielleure spent a year testing his trading strategy before going out on his own. And even though his colleagues sometimes urged him to take bigger risks, he kept his positions small. Similarly, Lo kept the bulk of her capital in treasuries and traded a relatively small portfolio in the futures market – a market she thoroughly understood. Adhering religiously to the tenets of day trading, she tended to hold positions in the futures contracts she traded for just minutes at a time. And she dutifully went flat each night.

Trading conservatively, using small amounts of cash, is especially important after suffering a setback, each of the 12 traders advised. Successfully taking small positions helps rebuild confidence, Velez teaches his students. Bruce arrived at essentially the same conclusion. By taking small positions and setting a small goal of $200 profit for himself each day, he steadily rebuilt his account.

Rule number 2: Stay close to the market

Time and again the traders I spoke with stressed the need to focus on the market each and every day. Even on days when they did no trading whatsoever, most stayed close to their screens, e-mailing fellow traders, while CNBC played on their TV monitors. Bob Martin and Scott McCormick both hold down full-time jobs, but they too make a habit of reviewing their positions at the end of each day. By watching the markets every day, several traders remarked they were able to develop an almost Zen-like sense of where prices were headed. That kind of intuition, they insisted, was vital to their success.

Rule number 3: Load up on tech

While a few traders would occasionally put their money into sectors such as restaurants and energy companies, the great majority kept their holdings in tech. Lo and Farrell were the notable exceptions. Lo, as noted, traded futures contracts on the S&P 100, and Farrell traded debt hybrids. As for the rest, their preference for tech is obvious. In the bull market, tech was where you needed to go to find high growth. In bearish times, tech provided the volatility short-term traders needed to eke profits from a directionless market. Tech stocks were also the vehicles of choice for traders placing long-term bets. Martin spent a lot of time searching for his gorilla stocks. But once he opened a position, he tended to stick with it. However, he and other traders also advised diversifying holdings within the tech sector – buying stocks of hardware companies. Internet companies, wireless and telecommunications companies, for instance, as different sectors were bound to go through cyclical turns.

Rule number 4: Create a watch list

To find their stocks, our traders used a variety of methods. Dave Gordon looked at news events and often came across the names of winning companies hidden deep within press releases. Martin got some of his recommendations from the Gorilla and King Portfolio Candidate message board on Silicon Investor. Barbara Simon used an online stock screening service to find companies with strong earnings potential.

Regardless of how the stocks were found, all the traders were diligent about maintaining lists of the stocks they chose to actively follow. Scott McCormick ran his watch list through complex technical and neural net screens each evening. Oliver Velez pored over charts of the companies he watched. Watch lists vary in size depending on the trader. Simon had about 50 stocks on her A-list. Scott McCormick's list might number well over one hundred stocks.

With a watch list duly set up, traders could then set about analyzing their companies further. Some, like Martin, did his through fundamental analysis. Others like Velez, looked for specific candlestick chart patterns to emerge. DeLamielleure put his watch list on a real-time ticker so he could watch prices change in the course of daily trading. If one of his stocks made an unusual move, he would zoom in, look at the chart, and hope he'd found a trading opportunity.

Rule number 5: Set rules, but know when to break them

The most successful traders in this book were those who could clearly articulate the rules they followed when they traded. And that fact, in itself, constitutes one of this book's most valuable lessons. Many of the traders felt so strongly about their rules, they took the time to write them out. An example of a rule might be something like this: "If a stock trades down to its 100-day moving average on low volume, I see an impending reversal and a possible buying opportunity." Or, "I only invest in stocks that received the highest recommendation from *Investor's Business Daily*." Or, "I only hold positions overnight if the market sells off slightly at the close after posting heavy gains for the day." In essence, rules tend to be a series of conditions stocks or markets as a whole were required to meet before these traders would act. All the traders in this book felt rules were crucial in that they gave the traders both a framework and a sense of discipline.

That said, markets continually change. And the best traders were those able to recognize that they must change their rules. When DeLamielleure determined that stocks weren't behaving the way he'd predicted, he

> **" The most successful traders in this book were those who could clearly articulate the rules they followed when they traded. And that fact, in itself, constitutes one of this book's most valuable lessons. Many of the traders felt so strongly about their rules, they took the time to write them out. "**

went back to the drawing board, so to speak, by studying the investment methods of book author Robert Deel. Deel used a charting method similar to the one DeLamielleure himself used.

Rule number 6: Determine the number of open positions you're comfortable holding

The number of open positions traders preferred seemed to depend on how intensely they traded each stock. For example, Lo traded only one thing day after day, e-mini contracts on the S&P 100. "Trade only one thing, but trade it intensely," she is fond of saying. Likewise, Chris Farrell, trading in the slow-moving debt hybrid market, might keep only four positions open at a given time. Why so few? Because his strategy depends on minute fractional gains, he must be able to constantly monitor his positions and stand ready to trade in or out at the first sign of even the slightest blip in price. By contrast, long-term trader Bob Martin sought to diversify as much as practical within his select technology stock picks. And he might hold dozens of positions at a time.

Rule number 7: Use a limited number of indicators, but know them intimately

All of us who trade the markets are exposed to an inordinate amount of noise: newspaper articles, countless e-mail newsletters from financial Web sites, never-ending commentary from guests and hosts on CNBC. Add to that an often-confusing barrage of cryptic technical indicators. All of it – the news, the technical indicators – supposedly serves as a barometer of the market. But more often it amounts to information overload and leads to paralysis by analysis. At the other extreme, the risk is equally great – namely that we will pick out one isolated bit of information and trade on it, without thoroughly thinking it through. More often than not, such shoot-from-the-hip trades wind up losing money. Worse, they cause us to veer from our trading plan.

All traders must at some point come to grips with the problem of information overload. Each of the successful traders in this book developed techniques for filtering the information they received. Teresa Lo says that when she loses her sense of the market's direction she tries to hone her focus down to just two indicators: price and volume. With a similar goal in mind, Bob Martin tends to do copious amount of research on the stocks he thinks will be long-term winners and the sectors to which they belong. However, once he reaches a decision over what to buy, he is normally content to ride out periods of short-term volatility – filtering out the short-term market noise, in other words – because he is confident his picks will come through for him in the end.

So which indicators proved most popular among these traders? Several paid close attention to moving averages. But each chose different time frames. Dave Gordon chose a 13-day moving average, for example, while Brendan DeLamielleure honed in on a 5-minute tick chart.

Rule number 8: Buy on dips

The only way to make money in the markets, of course is to buy low and sell high. That is, unless you are a short seller in which case you sell high and buy back lower. But as it happened, the traders in this book didn't make shorting a major part of their strategy. What they did practice universally was buying on dips. Meaning, they took advantage of short-term price reversals in order to accumulate shares. And they did this regardless of their trading time frame. Recall that Mary Pugh, who held positions longer than any other trader in this book, got her start by scooping up Microsoft shares whenever bad news about the company came out. Oliver Velez used candlestick charts to detect price reversals that identified swing trading opportunities. By studying the candlestick patterns nightly over a period of years, he was able to readily decipher their many nuances. Still other traders found buying opportunities when shares drifted below a moving average on low volume. Brendan DeLamielleure had perhaps the most sophisticated tactic of all. Even as stocks trended downward, they occasionally reversed for brief intraday periods. DeLamielleure identified those temporary halts in a stock's decline, bought shares and then rode them up, either over the course of the day or of several days.

Rule number 9: Let the market come to you

This rule is another way of saying plan your trades and then trade your plan. Several traders, among them Velez, McCormick, Simon, and Pugh, described in detail how they identified trading opportunities and then set target entry and exit points. If the market failed to meet their entry price, they often put off the trade and looked for other opportunities.

Rule number 10: When the market turns choppy, shorten your trading horizon

As has been noted several times, this book chronicles traders' progress during two critical market time frames: the bull run of '98 to early 2000 and the choppy aftermath that ensued from April 2000 onward. Each species of market required markedly different trading tactics. To be sure, huge losses were possible during the bull market, as mini-corrections could pare 10 percent or more off a stock's value. But these price fluctuations normally occurred over a period of days. This enabled traders like Simon and others to employ swing trading strategies, holding positions overnight, and allowing stocks to vacillate within a fairly wide range before reaching their target exit price. The crash of 2000 forced these traders to radically change their tactics. As markets rose and fell chaotically, the traders focused on the only time frame in which they could discern a clear trend. In other words, they had to hone their focus to hours and sometimes minutes. If they held longer term, they adjusted their stops or at least their mental entry and exit points to reflect the increased intraday volatility. Those traders who failed to change their strategies to meet the bear market continued to suffer losses.

Rule number 11: Build a core position and trade around it

This technique allowed several traders to accelerate gains and cap losses. You'll recall how it works: Just as traders built watch lists of stocks they paid close attention to, they also created an even shorter list – the stock that formed part of their portfolio. These of course, tended to be stocks they were intimately familiar with. In some cases, traders knew the companies' fundamentals cold. In other cases they were well versed in the stocks' trading ranges. More often than not, they were familiar with both the technical indicators and the fundamentals. This allowed them to add to losing positions with relative safety in order to minimize losses – the technique known as "averaging down."

Alternately, they were able to build on gains they'd already made by adding shares as a stock rose in price. They averaged up, in other words. (Lo was one trader dead set against averaging up.)

Trading around a core position also enabled those interviewed to preserve gains or cut losses when they were less certain where a stock was headed. For example, if they bought a stock only to see it fall, they might sell part of their position and hold the other half, in the hope that the stock would eventually rise. Similarly, if they bought a stock that did indeed rise, they might sell enough to cover the stock's initial purchase price. If the shares that remained continued to rise, they would produce additional profit. If they fell in price, the trader would at worst break even on the trade.

Rule number 12: Back your winners, cut your losers

This rule is similar to number 11. Once they'd calculated the risks and potential rewards of holding a position, the most successful traders in this book had clearly established points where they would exit losing trades. They knew they must be willing to take their losses and move on. The less successful traders in this book did not follow this rule. The harsh truth is that many of those who sustained deep pain during the April 2000 dot-com bomb did so because they held on to positions for too long.

As a group, traders appeared less focused on when they should exit winning trades. Those with a longer-term perspective would continue to hold on to stocks as long as they continued rising, and even add to those positions if circumstances warranted. Bob Martin described this as "the Russian Army approach" to investing. The term applies to a seemingly cruel tactic used by Russian generals during World War II: Faced with limited resources, the generals were generous in furnishing supplies to those armies that could show gains against the Nazis. Armies that were less successful were left to fend for themselves.

Significantly, other traders in this book eschewed this approach. Their style matched that of guerrilla fighters. They were content to take small gains as a stock rolled up in price. The expectation was that the stock, having gone up, was now ripe for a temporary reversal. Rather than hold on to the stock for the long term, they searched out better short-term opportunities among other stocks. When their original stock did reverse downward, they might once again buy shares and ride the stock up for a second time.

Rule number 13: Trade small positions aggressively while keeping the bulk of your trades in safer investments

By trading small amounts we all become better traders. For proof of that just visit any of the numerous online trading contests such CNet's (www.cnet.com) "The Game." The top finishers each month always seem to have incredibly high returns. But there is an easy explanation for this. Since they are in effect wagering nothing, they can afford to risk everything. Some of the best traders in this book employed a similar philosophy – although unlike the game players, they used real money, just relatively small amounts. Teresa Lo, for example, wisely stashed the bulk of the profits she'd made through high-risk trades into ultra-conservative investments such as treasuries. This allowed her to focus closely on the trading vehicle she specialized in, S&P futures. DeLamielleure followed the same strategy. On any given day, the bulk of his account would be in cash earning interest. While he traded only a small portion of his account, the rest was at the ready should an unusual opportunity arise. By intensely trading a few select stocks, he says he was able to earn $2,500 on average each day. Bob Martin opted for safety and moderate income when he sold deep-in-the-money calls on his gorilla stocks. Because the calls were deep in the money, they offered plenty of "insurance" or downside protection in the event the stock declined. Meanwhile, premiums from the sales of the calls generated income. And he could opt to use that income to finance trades with a relatively higher degree of risk.

Rule number 14: Devise a strategy that suits your personality

This is perhaps the most important rule of all. And it's the one successful traders are best at following. Successful trading styles were those that took advantage of people's natural strengths. Mary Pugh, for example, describes herself as analytical. She can look at the numbers on a company's balance sheet, examine its products, and then predict what its future revenues might be. Holding long-term positions in promising young companies seems like a natural outgrowth of her personality. Bob Martin used his lawyer's analytical mind to study companies in much the same manner. By contrast, both Chris Farrell and Brendan DeLamielleure spent time at brokerage houses trading desks. Their short-term trading strategies were natural outgrowths of their experiences there.

Trader personalities: a close-up view

Now let's look more closely at what made these traders tick – specifically those personality traits that either hindered or helped their success. And obviously, all of this is based on my own impressions. No science here. But maybe some food for thought, nonetheless.

Let's maybe start by focusing on the one thing these traders were not. It would be tempting to conclude that the 12 traders in the book possessed a natural risk-taking or gambling mentality. But this was far from true. Only Dave Gordon told me that before he became involved with stocks, he used to enjoy the occasional bet at the horse track. But on the whole, traders took great pains to minimize risks. As noted earlier, Brendan DeLamielleure's trading buddies often pointed to his consistent relatively smallish gains, saying they were proof he wasn't taking large enough risks. And finally there's Bob Martin, who put his entire portfolio in tech stocks (and did the same with the portfolio of his 70-year-old mother!) However, high returns weren't his chief reason, he says. Martin reasoned that over the long term, those stocks – issued by companies that were redesigning our economy – were the safest of all places to put his money.

So if they weren't gamblers, what were they? One clue comes from something several told me – namely that they'd spent a long time searching for a trading strategy until they found one that best suited them. Oliver Velez describes his long study of technical analysis as "a kind of quest." Similarly, Mary Pugh – while discovering early on that she had analytical abilities and that she was a natural-born contrarian – nevertheless experimented with several other trading strategies, such as day trading and short selling, before settling on her current course, which is to find undiscovered small companies with huge upside potential. Before settling on futures trading, Teresa Lo dabbled in everything from long options to penny mining stocks.

So perhaps it would be accurate to say that they were deeply motivated, and in some cases even scholarly in their pursuit of market knowledge. It's notable that in their search for the ultimate trading strategy, quite a few traders took advice from mentors. Oliver Velez was influenced by trader/psychologist Dr. Alexander Elder. DeLamielleure learned a few lessons from Robert Deel. Both Barbara Hamilton and Bob Martin studied the predictions of Internet stock guru Steve Harmon. And Dave Gordon used to exchange late night e-mails with TheStreet.com's co-founder James Cramer.

As with all students, the traders in this book assimilated and adapted the knowledge from these gurus into their own trading strategies. In fact, many went on to become teachers themselves. Velez set up several companies that train active traders. Slutsky, Lo, Simon, and Gordon all operate online trading rooms where participants take part in live chat. Mary Pugh, for her part, is among the most active posters on the financial chat site RagingBull.com. Chris Farrell was in the process of setting up a trading room as this book went to press. Likewise, McCormick was completing work on his Web site FundPilot.com, an advisory service for mutual fund investors.

Besides giving them the chance to offer advice, many saw their trading rooms as a means of social interaction. It can get boring watching market data by yourself all day, Lo complained. But something deeper appears to be at work here, something that offers yet another clue to these traders' personalities. There seemed a need for traders to share their knowledge and to build something that encompassed more than just trading profits. It suggests that as an activity, trading alone is not sufficiently fulfilling. Despite the potential for enormous gain, despite the daily drama of watching markets seesaw, and despite the intellectual stimulation that comes from dissecting company financials or news events or deciphering intricate chart patterns, traders sought additional outlets for their talents. In fact, this phenomenon is quite common. There is, after all, a huge industry built around assisting people as they learn to trade or invest (one that the author readily admits to being a part of). Often people wonder – justifiably so – "If these teachers were so good why would they share what they know? Why wouldn't they just go into their home offices and make their millions?"

Perhaps this need to teach explains part of it. Or this need to escape the isolation that particularly afflicts at-home traders. "When I take money out of the market, it doesn't do anything for me spiritually," one successful trader who is not in this book told me. "My real sense of fulfilment comes from teaching others how to trade."

" They also discovered trading to be a kind of ultimate creative game. Each day they matched wits with some of the smartest people on the planet. Each day the game proved slightly different. Each day their skills were tested to the limit. "

All work and no play

An aversion to risk, a deep desire to learn, and a subsequent need to teach: What other personality traits did these traders possess? All were motivated and successful. All worked hard, to be sure. As hard as they would have if they held down a stressful job. And indeed, several displayed near workaholic habits as they described to me spending the day trading and their nights studying up on charts. Alas, the capacity for hard work made some of the traders' lives appear one-dimensional at times. Many were somewhat vague about their activities when not trading. A few spoke of exercising as a way to relive stress. Others spoke of travelling. But often this was to attend shows devoted to trading or to visit trader colleagues.

Nevertheless, thanks to their work habits, you could safely predict that each would have achieved success in whatever field they might have chosen. And in fact, all the traders enjoyed successful careers prior to taking up trading. Terry Bruce owned a thriving photography business; Teresa Lo could have continued her success working for a broker. Scott McCormick, Bob Martin, and Oliver Velez continue to hold down high-level jobs. Recall that Dave Gordon owned a swimming pool business. It was illness that prompted him to take up trading. The new career allowed him to make the money he needed while he recovered at home.

Many remarked that they took up trading because it offered freedom and flexibility. They also discovered trading to be a kind of ultimate creative game. Each day they matched wits with some of the smartest people on the planet. Each day the game proved slightly different. Each day their skills were tested to the limit. Several mentioned that for precisely these reasons they looked forward to the start of each day.

Trading also gave them the chance to earn substantially more than they might have in their old careers. Barbara Hamilton told me that early on in her trading career she managed to make more money in six months of playing the market than her day job paid her in an entire year. Months later, as the market rose, she found herself making more in a single day than she had in a whole year as a computer programmer. Then a few months later, she found herself losing a month or even a year's salary in the course of a day.

Becoming players

Which brings up another trait all these traders appeared to have in common: All had faced huge losses in the past. Teresa Lo, one the most successful traders in the book, and Terry Bruce both lost all of their trading capital. Mary Pugh lost the greatest sum – $6 million. Yet rather than throwing in the towel, they resolved to try trading once more.

Dwelling on such huge losses would drive anyone nuts. So these traders learned to think of money in abstract terms – just as those who teach day trades often advise. Also the more successful traders resolved to learn from their mistakes. Some, like Bruce, returned to the market trading small amounts. Others focused their strategies when they found their old tactics weren't working any longer.

At the start of this section on traders' personalities, I noted my belief that none were risk takers by nature. But that doesn't mean they refused to take risks when taking risks was deemed necessary – only that they seek to minimize risks. Most traders talked about taking huge risks in their early years. "Before I knew better," was a typical comment. It was these very risks that enabled them to build their trading accounts. Like entrepreneurs or politicians or anyone else who has achieved success in our society, without the risk, these traders wouldn't be where they are today. In other words, no guts, no glory!

Appendix
Money for Nothing and the Quotes Are Free
Understanding the basics of day trading

Before online investing brought about a low-commission revolution, day trading was restricted to a wealthy few who could afford the price of a seat on a major exchange. Now the price of admission is a round-trip commission of $25 or less. And that commission keeps dropping.

Today's arrhythmic markets only add to day trading's appeal. Who can resist the occasional gamble on volatile Internet stocks like CMGI, or Siebel Systems (SEBL), or JDS Uniphase (JDSU) – all favorites among day traders – when they move 5, 10, or 20 more percentage points in a single day? Buy the stock in the morning. Watch the price fluctuate tick by tick on your computer screen. Sell the moment you think the stock's price has peaked. And pocket a few hundred in profits as you search the market for new opportunities. Some day traders will only hold positions during market hours and revert their accounts to cash at the close. Others may keep a stock for several days or even weeks. As long as it continues to rise.

If this makes day trading sound easy, be forewarned: It's not – although you can probably understand why thousands of people have given day trading a try. Estimates of the number of day traders plying their craft at any given time tend to vary. Mark Erzhorn, editor of the new magazine *Active Trader*, for example, puts their number at 100,000. A study by the investment bank Robertson Stephens claims some 800,000 traders make at least 10 trades per month. And in the process they account for half of all the trades recorded by the major U.S. exchanges.

Needless to say, there's considerable churn among active day traders. Most lose money – at least when they begin. As inexperienced traders get blown out, new ones stand ready to take their places. The battle-hardened survivors average anywhere from $500 to $2,500 per day. And the really phenomenal traders earn many times that.

What does it take to survive, or better yet, thrive as a day trader? For starters, a 500 megahertz or better computer with a fast Internet connection and a broker who specializes in day trading. That's the easy part: The hard part is learning to pick stocks and mastering the adept plays day traders use. And then there are still more difficult obstacles, namely developing the discipline and nerve that it takes to succeed.

Want to learn how to day trade? Consider the steps outlined here as well as the strategies of the successful traders profiled in this book as a kind of introductory lecture. To really stand a chance of success you should read every book on the subject you can lay your hands on. Follow the market every day, and – perhaps – try paper trading to see just how well your ideas work.

Day trading tools

Chips for the game

Day traders speak reverently about their "capital" – the pile of money they use to invest. It's what keeps them in business. A few bad trades and suddenly you're a telemarketer. So the more capital, the better. Some say as little as $20,000. You'll have to trade that amount on margin of course. Which means your broker will consider your $20,000 as collateral and loan you an additional 20 grand, giving you $40,000 in effective buying power. This doubles any gains you make, just as it double yours losses.

Even if you leverage your $20,000 via a margin account, we're not talking about a great deal of money here. Some traders say it's feasible to earn a living with just 20 grand, because so many stocks move crazily up and down that you can make your money on their daily ranges. Other more conservative traders say you need as much as $100,000. Anything less, they say, and a couple of mistakes will blow out your account. At the other extreme, some day trading brokerages let you open accounts with just a few thousand. The norm for beginners is roughly $50,000. And again, some would insist that you must routinely trade that amount of margin in order to be successful.

In truth, the amount of money you put in the market will dictate the kinds of stocks you can buy. Remember, you'll want to purchase 1,000-share lots in order to profit from ⅛-point moves. *Ergo*, $20,000 invested on margin will buy up to 1,000 shares of a $40 stock. Whereas, you'd need $100,000 on margin to trade biotech index shares like Biotech HLDRs (BBH), for example. Moreover, many day traders like to maintain two or more open positions simultaneously – which, of course, requires still more cash.

As any reputable broker will tell you: Never trade with money that you need to live on – so no maxing out your credit cards or taking out a home equity loan. Likewise, lots of Americans have amassed $20,000 or more via 401(k)s, IRAs, and the like. Trading these tax-free funds has its drawbacks, however. When it comes to retirement accounts, the IRS forbids buying on margin or short selling, and most brokerages only allow highly conservative options hedging strategies.

Of course, you could cash out of your IRA, pay the 10 percent tax penalty, and declare the money as income. But that too, would be highly imprudent. Ideally, you want to trade with some other form of savings. More fortunate day traders use their tax-free accounts for long-term investments in growth-oriented stocks, while aggressively day trading other funds.

Hardware and communications

A day-trading nightmare occurs when a stock takes a freefall. You try to get out when .... *your computer bombs!*

Little wonder day traders opt for reliability and redundancy when they choose a PC. (Alas, very little serious trading software exists for Macs.) In fact, most traders I've spoken with use two or more computers – one for hooking up to a chat room or news service, the other for their actual trades. Both computers should be 500 megahertz or better, and ideally hooked up to a failsafe power source to protect against outages.

Load up each computer with a minimum 128 megs of memory. This will allow you to safely keep several windows open on the screen at once – which is something day trading software calls for, as you'll see. Likewise, because you'll want to be looking at several windows at once, it pays to invest in a large-screen monitor – 21 inches is ideal.

High-end day trading computer systems are the stuff of computer geek fantasies. Some incorporate four or more computer monitors. That gives you enough real estate to track half a dozen different stocks and market indices at once. As for operating systems: Windows 2000 Professional edition lets you run multiple monitors, and it's more fault-tolerant than its problem-plagued consumer cousin, Windows 98.

Many day traders like to put their computer systems in a room with a cable hook-up and a TV monitor. That way you can keep tabs on CNNfn or CNBC. Both networks move stocks just by mentioning them. Plan on shelling out for satellite TV if you want both networks, however.

Connections

Note we haven't said anything yet about modems or Internet service providers. Here, your choice might depend on the day trading broker you sign with. A few brokers offer direct connections via a private network. The technology, called "frame-relay," neatly avoids Internet bottlenecks and may give you priority access to your broker's servers. But you'll pay a hefty bill of about $1,000 per month, or the same as you'd pay for a T1 Internet connection.

An alternative would be to invest in a cable modem or digital subscriber line (DSL) if either service is available where you live. Expect to pay $40 or more per month for either. And in the case of DSL, that's on top of your ISP's regular monthly charge.

Better yet, make that two ISP charges. Many day traders recommend having two separate ISP accounts. That way, if one service goes down, you have a back-up. Some also recommend having two separate phone lines, one for your dial-up connection the other so you can call your broker, shrink or spiritual advisor during moments of extreme angst. Bottom line: Expect your communications bill to run $120 or more per month.

Direct access brokers

Online trading showed us that we don't have to wait half a day for our broker to get back to us in order to execute a trade. You can buy into that rapidly rising telco stock as quickly as you can log on.

So-called direct access brokers that cater to day traders add yet another warp factor to the speed equation. They provide users with high-speed trading-software suites that include things like real-time chart-building capabilities and Level II quote screens. Perhaps most important, direct access brokerages provide instant executions via either electronic communications networks (ECNs), NASDAQ's Small Order Execution System (SOES), or the Designated Order Turn-around (DOT) system used by the NYSE.

We'll get into the specialized software and the Level II quotes in a moment. But before that, it helps to know why ECNs like Island.com can save substantial amounts of money.

Let's look at how a trade takes place when you use a "traditional" online broker. You log into your brokerage account. Enter your order, and probably re-enter your password to confirm it. Now comes the interesting part. Your brokerage may itself take the other side of your trade. Alternately, it may route your order to either a market maker on the NASDAQ exchange or one of the specialists who work at the NYSE, depending on where the stock trades.

Both market makers and specialists act as exchange-sanctioned wholesalers. They guarantee that there will always be someone on the other end to buy or sell your stock. Market makers and specialists buy stocks at the bid price and sell them at the ask price. And they make money by the spread or price difference between the bid and ask.

The more volume these wholesalers generate, the more money they make. Which is why market makers will pay brokerages a few cents a share in commission for every customer order they receive. In the investing world, this is called "payment for order flow." It's a controversial practice. But it's widespread, nonetheless.

Below wholesale!

Indeed, payment for order flow is the reason online brokerages are able to charge such low commissions. You place a market order for 1,000 shares of Echelon Corp. (ELON), currently selling at around $30. You pay your broker a $10 commission. Your online broker may also receive $20 or a 2-cent-per-share payment from the market maker. In some cases, market makers have been known to wait a few moments for the stock's price to rise – say $1/8$ of a point – before filling your order. When that happens the market maker receives $125 for your 1,000-share market order – what amounts to a hidden commission.

True enough, you can protect yourself from this hidden commission charge by only using limit orders, where you specify the price at which you're willing to buy or sell the shares. But here again, market makers have been known to sit on limit orders until a price moves favorably in their direction.

And that's often why trades can take several minutes to be executed. Losing $\frac{1}{8}$ of a point means little when you plan to hold the stock till retirement. But for day traders, who think and act in seconds a $\frac{1}{8}$-point spread means the difference between a money-making or money-losing trade.

By contrast, when a day trading brokerage routes your order through an ECN, your bid or ask is broadcast for traders everywhere to see on their screens. If someone out there meets your price, the trade occurs instantly. And often this means you can get inside the bid and ask spread.

Trading software

The software that direct access brokerages use speeds up the process in other ways, too. Remember that you'll be linked up to your direct access broker either directly or via a high-speed Internet connection. Either way, the broker's day trading software streams quote data directly to your desktop. That's a lot faster than waiting for your broker's Web server to first build a page and then transmit it to you over the Internet, particularly if thousands of other customers are requesting pages at the same time you are.

Meanwhile, all the processing power resides on your desktop PC. And it's that software that takes the raw data feed your broker sends out and constructs real-time charts and tickers. Day traders like to have multiple windows on their screens to watch real-time quotes and charts while keeping their eyes on news feeds. Expert systems embedded in day trading software may suggest entry and exit points as stock prices fluctuate. You can choose the ECN you want to use to route your order with a single keystroke.

Day trading software doesn't come cheap. Online brokerages rent their programs for upward of $250 per month. Add another $80 per month for real-time NASDAQ quotes, and another $75 per month for news fees. But brokerages typically waive all but the newswire fee for traders who make 40 or so trades per month.

At present, a handful of day trading programs exist: RealTickIII, Watcher, CyBerTrader, and TradeCast are some of the better known brands. The software you use will depend on the brokerage you sign with. In some cases, brokerages add their own nameplate to the programs – with videogame monikers like The Executioner or TORS.

Why you absolutely need Level II quotes

Some day traders insist it's better to get your data feeds and your order routing from two different sources. In other words, sign with a direct access broker, and use that broker solely to enter order entry. Use a third-party quote provider such as eSignal or Window on Wall Street for your Level II data services. According to this reasoning, third-party quote providers make offering fast, reliable data feeds their top priority. And they usually add new features faster than do brokerages. And it's always easier to change quote providers than it is to move your portfolio to a different broker. For their part, direct access brokers are primarily interested in order routing.

Wherever you go to get your Level II quotes, know that day trading effectively is next to impossible without them. Sure, you say, aren't there plenty of Level I real-time quote services available free on the Web? Absolutely, but these only show the highest bid or the lowest offer, and the number of shares put up at that price.

By contrast, Level II quotes show all the offers from major market makers as well as ECNs. They're all ranked neatly on the screen by price. Watching the prices and quantities change – knowing whether the offer's being made by Merrill Lynch or Smith Barney or a day trader using the Island ECN – is how day traders deduce when an issue is poised for a move. For example: A wide spread between the high and low bid price for a stock often signals a lack of buying pressure. However, if the spread suddenly narrows, it could be a signal to buy in anticipation of a price jump.

Learn before you earn

Using Level II trading software effectively takes time. Some direct access brokerages such as CyBerCorp.com allow you to practice by paper trading for a couple of months. Paper trading has at least two serious drawbacks, however. You can't be sure you would have actually gotten in or out at the price you specified. Neither can you be certain you'd have had the nerve if the money you put in play was real. Rule of thumb: Take any of the results you receive from paper trading and deduct at least 20 percent. That amount will more closely approximate what you can expect by trading with real money.

School of hard knocks

As a next step, day trading brokerages offer courses on how to use their software. In some cases, you take the training at the brokerage's headquarters. In other cases, you can train online. The courses don't come cheap, however. Expect to pay several thousand for few intensive days of practice.

Enrolling in day trading boot camp will likely tell you whether you're cut out to risk your life savings in the market day after day. Part of successful day trading involves keeping your cool, even in the face of huge losses. Some day trading schools urge their students not to think of losses in terms of dollars – but rather points. You need that kind of detachment if you're planning on returning to the market and trading with confidence a day after you've received a serious drubbing. You also need certain shoot-from-the-hip skills. If you analyze trades for too long the opportunity will be lost. For this reason, some say that engineers – whose profession demands that they be analytical – make poor day traders. Pilots, on the other hand, are trained to react quickly when necessary. And those skills translate well to day trading.

Your trading style

To day trade successfully you need to find a trading style that suits you, veterans advise. As one trader succinctly put it, "You really have to find a style that fits into your emotional set-up as a trader, your tolerance of pain, your risk-reward, your mental state of discipline. And your equity, of course."

So what exactly is a trading style? Think of it as an amalgamation of several things. It's choosing the stocks you wish to trade and getting to know them intimately – say, by studying their intraday charts until you begin to see repeating patterns. It's practicing and honing a few trading strategies the way you might practice your tennis serve or golf swing. And it's developing certain rules that you trade by and sticking to them. Successful traders also advise keeping a diary so you can look back on why certain trades worked and why others bombed. Beyond that, they draw from the axioms, trading tactics, and rules we've listed here.

The basics

Day trading is really all about getting in and out of stocks quickly in order to take advantage of minute price moves. So learning exactly how the stocks you trade move is fundamental. Indeed, all stocks tend to move up or down in predictable increments of, say $\frac{1}{4}$, $\frac{1}{8}$ or $\frac{1}{16}$ of a point. Day traders call these increments "levels." The number of levels a stock moves during an average day is called its "range." And because day traders hold positions for only seconds at a time, they pay more attention to levels and ranges than they do the actual price.

For example, if the stock of ABC Corp. trades between 120 and 121½ points, its range is 1½ points. Therefore, if it falls to 119, expect it to rise to 120½. Knowing that a stock trades in a 1½-point range helps you know when it's time to get in and out during upward and downward moves.

Ideally, a stock's daily range should be 5 times the average spread between its bid and ask price. A range like that will likely attract many day traders. And eventually the buying and selling by day traders inside the range will cause the range to narrow – to the point where the stock is no longer profitable to trade.

Occasionally, however, a stock may break out of its trading range and uptrend or downtrend. Perhaps an institution's accumulating the stock, or it's been hit by a couple of analyst downgrades. Before entering any trade, decide if a stock is within a trading range, an uptrend, or a downtrend. Look for such things as volume, institutional interest, and short interest.

Choosing stocks

- *Avoid highly volatile, household-name Internet stocks*: You know: the Amazons, the e-Bays. You can be sure the best market makers and day traders are lurking around these stocks. Those guys are your competition, so stay clear until you've gotten some experience.

- *Go where the action is (or isn't)*: Look for stocks trading 2-4 times average volume and moving up or down 5 to 10 percent. Short stocks that are significantly underperforming the S&P. Alternately buy stocks within indexes that are significantly outperforming the S&P on the day. Weak stocks within uptrending indexes are a good bet when they're rising in price on higher than normal volume. This can mean that major sellers have been taken out or that fresh buyers are heading in.

- *Find stocks linked to indicators and trade on movements in those indicators*: For example, banks and other interest-rate-sensitive stocks often move in tandem with bond prices. Lower bond prices = higher interest rates = lower bank stocks. Likewise oil price rises push down transport stocks. Export-oriented companies and those with significant overseas operations fall in price each time the dollar rises. But retail stocks, especially retailers that sell imported goods such as electronics, rise along with the dollar.

- *Look at general market indicators to confirm the trend*: The NASDAQ, Dow, and S&P averages, the tick on the S&P, bond prices, advancers versus decliners, and new highs versus new lows. If all are up, it's generally better to go long. If all are down it's generally better to go short.

Trading strategies

- *Post-opening buying*: Let's say a stock rises 5 percent or more during the opening and there's no news about it. Typically, the stock will fall off after 30 minutes of trading. Why? Market makers may be trying to open the stock at an artificially high price to sell off excess inventory they've acquired the day before. However, if the stock doesn't fall after 30 minutes of trading, it's liable to continue rising for the rest of the day. Tactic: Buy at $1/16$ above the day's high and after the opening. Set a stop $1/16$ below the day's low.

- *Post-opening selling*: Here's the opposite of the previous strategy. When a stock opens lower on no news, it could be that sell orders from nervous investors have piled up since the close of trading the day before. Sometimes market makers open the stock artificially low, to draw in more panic sellers. This allows them to accumulate shares, since market makers as a rule buy on price declines and sell on price increases. After 30 minutes, the stock usually recovers in price and normal trading begins. The market makers profit by selling the inventory they've accumulated by taking advantage of the lower price. However, if the stock continues to drift lower after 30 minutes, chances are it'll decline more during the course of the day. Tactic: Sell short at $1/16$ below the low of the day; set a stop at $1/16$ above the day's high.

- *Playing the spread*: This one's really simple. Buy at $1/16$ above the bid. Sell at $1/16$ below the ask. The strategy works best with non-volatile stocks where the spread is at least $3/8$ of a point. When successful, you make $1/4$ point per trade, or $250 on 1,000 shares. You can also short the spread by selling short at $1/16$ below the ask and covering at $1/16$ above the bid. Problem is, it's not always possible to get in and out at these levels. Market makers may easily spot what you're doing and adjust prices so they blow you out. Often day traders try this tactic several times during the day before they succeed.

- *Grinding*: Another relatively simple tactic. Follow the message threads for a particular stock at Silicon Investor, for example. When everyone is screaming that the stock is going to make a move, jump in with the mob. Only be content with ⅛ or ¼ point. Then get out before the rush.

- *Fading the market*: With this contrarian strategy, you buy into weakness and sell into strength. That is, you buy stocks with small percentage declines relative to the market. You're hoping they'll gain when the market reverses. Hold off buying until the stock trades above its opening. Reason: Previous buyers of the stock will sell to prevent loss, thus driving the price down in the short-term.

- *Shop the final hour*: Stocks often ease off their highs of the day during the last hour of trading. This occurs because day traders and market makers seek to exit their positions and lock in profits. This downward momentum can create some lucrative short-selling opportunities.

Cardinal rules

- *Don't go after windfalls*: Day traders insist they make their money through consistent small trades. The $250 you didn't make on Lucent (LU) can be made on Cisco Systems (CSCO) a minute from now. The market continually serves up new opportunities.

- *Don't overtrade*: Have a reason for each trade you enter. And be reasonably certain that you have an edge. Some say the hardest part of day trading is simply watching the screen and waiting for an opportunity to arise.

- *Ignore a company's fundamentals*: Earnings growth, return on equity, sales forecasts: They're all meaningless when you're holding a stock for only 30 seconds. Instead, assume – as technical analysts do – that everything about the stock is reflected in its price at that particular moment.

- *Be as comfortable going short as going long*: The goal is twofold: (1) Go with the trend, whatever that trend might be; and (2) Keep your capital working for you at all times.

- *Always have an exit strategy*: Decide at what price you'll sell a stock – for either a profit or a loss – before you actually buy it.

- *Don't average down*: That is, buy more shares to reduce your average cost basis when the stock has declined in value. This is a good tactic for longer-term investors but a lousy one for day traders.

- *Never try to time the market perfectly*: Some day traders buy and sell the same shares over and over again before they finally catch the breakout they want.

- *Never fight the trend*: The laws of inertia apply to the stock market just as they do to everything else. Stocks that rise in price tend to keep on rising. Stocks that decline will likely continue to decline.

- *Use stops, and move them in the direction of the trend*: A stop order automatically sells your stock when it reaches a specified price. As a stock's price increases, keep resetting the stop price a level or two below the bid. Short sellers follow a stock price down by resetting their stops one or two levels above the ask.

- *Preserve your capital*: Cut your losers immediately. Don't wish. Don't pray. Just get out.

- *Avoid trading when the market opens*: It's the most volatile time of the day. And only market makers know what buy and sell orders they've accumulated overnight. Wait 20-30 minutes after the bell, then trade.

- *Always "go flat" at the end of the day*: That is, never take positions overnight. Day traders allow that this rule is what enables then to sleep well at night. A possible exception: If you bought a stock near the close of the market that was trading up on the day and with high volume near the close. The stock will likely open higher the next day. Reason: Market makers may have sold the stock short to meet demand. They'll be quick to cover their positions the next day.

Index